NNAT

Naglieri Nonverbal Ability Test®

PATTERN
COMPLETION

A step by step STUDY GUIDE
GRADE 3

by MindMine

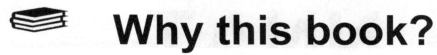 Why this book?

Cognitive abilities are brain-based skills related with the mechanisms of learning, memorizing, and paying attention rather than actual knowledge that was learned. **The more you practice, the more you develop** your cognitive flexibility.

- This book is designed to teach concepts and skills in a way kids understand with ease.

- Concepts are taught step by step and introduced incrementally.

- The focus of this book is to provide a solid foundation to fundamental skills. All the skills taught in the book will collectively increase the knowledge and will help kids to prepare and take the test confidently.

- Practice tests that are available in the market may not provide all the concepts needed. This book is aimed to give both concepts and practice.

Who should buy this book?

- 3rd graders taking NNAT test (NNAT2)

- 2nd graders planning to take NNAT (Any Form)

- 1st, 2nd and 3rd graders seeking to enrich their Nonverbal reasoning and Problem-solving skills

📚 What is covered?

This book extensively covers **PATTERN COMPLETION** section of **NNAT Test** with 180 unique questions and 200 secondary questions.

📚 **2 FULL LENGTH PRACTICE TESTS with Answers**

Full Length Practice Test#1	10 Questions
Full Length Practice Test#2	10 Questions

📚 **FUNDAMENTAL CONCEPTS**

📚 **PATTERN COMPLETION QUESTIONS**   180 Questions

📚 **ANSWERS**

📚 Table of Contents

Mind Mine

PATTERN COMPLETION

Question

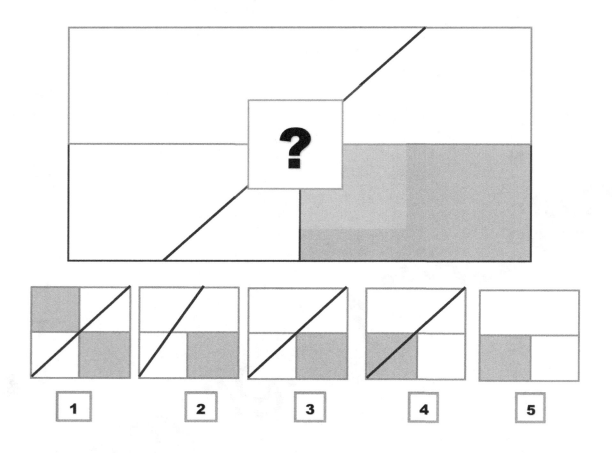

ANSWER: 3

2

PATTERN COMPLETION

HOW TO SOLVE?

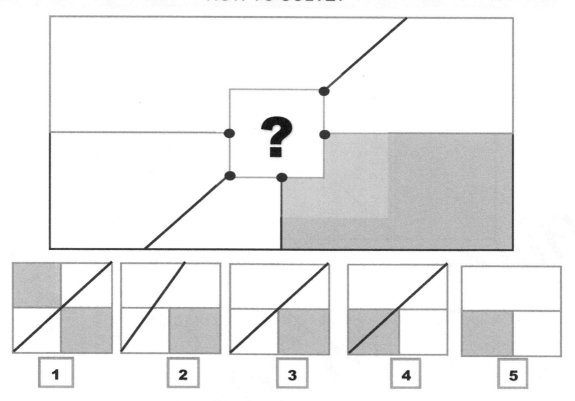

1	2	3	4	5

How to solve?

STEP-1: Understand given pattern

STEP-2: Identify all points where Box with question mark

(?) is intersecting with given pattern

STEP-3: Complete the pattern

NOTE: Pay attention to Color, Position, Pattern, Width, Thickness etc.,

STEP-4: Find the correct Answer

PATTERN COMPLETION

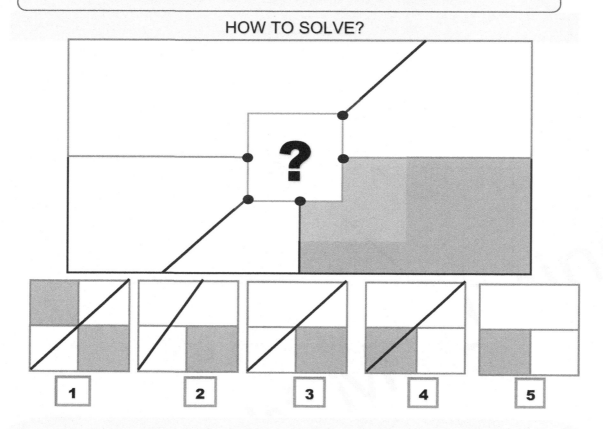

How to solve?

STEP-1: Understand given pattern

STEP-2: Identify all points where 'Box with question mark' (?) is intersecting with given pattern. Shown here with Black Dots (●).

STEP-3: Complete the pattern

STEP-4: ANSWER is 3

Answer 1 is incorrect. Top-Left box filled with Gray.

Answer 2 is incorrect. Line is Not intersecting Top-Right corner.

Answer 4 is incorrect. Bottom-Left box filled with Gray.

Answer 5 is incorrect. Line is missing. Bottom-Left box filled with Gray.

FILL PATTERN

PATTERN COMPLETION
Fill Pattern

Horizontal Lines Pattern

Vertical Lines Pattern

Diagonal Lines Pattern

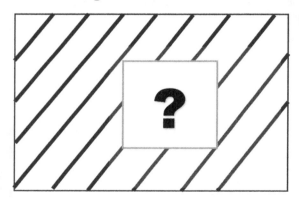

Diagonal Lines Pattern

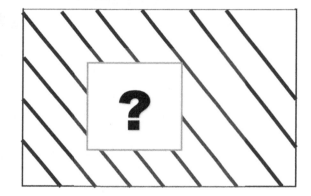

6

PATTERN COMPLETION
Fill Pattern

Lines with Dots

Broken Lines

Arrows (Left End Arrows)

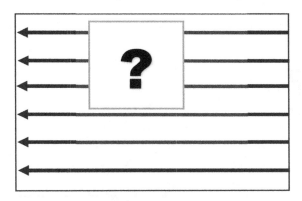

Arrows (Right End Arrows)

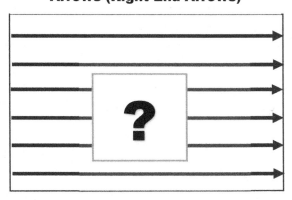

7

PATTERN COMPLETION
Fill Pattern

Arrows (Both Ends)

Arrows

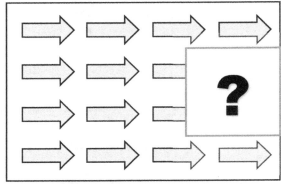

Arrows

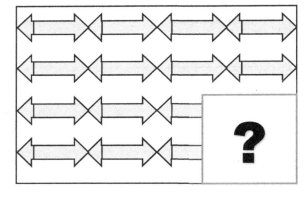

Arrows

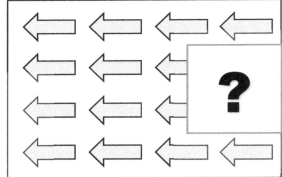

8

PATTERN COMPLETION
Fill Pattern

Lines with different patterns

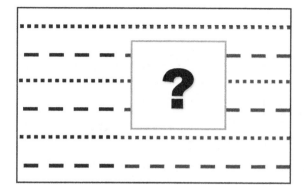

Lines with different patterns

Lines with different patterns

Lines with different patterns

PATTERN COMPLETION
Fill Pattern

Boxes Pattern

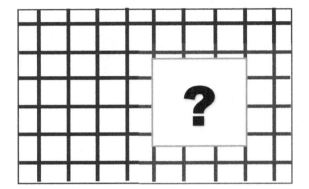

Squares Pattern

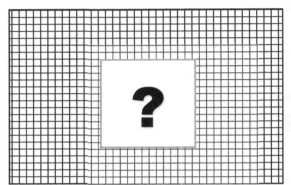

Dots Pattern

Diamonds Pattern

10

PATTERN COMPLETION
Fill Pattern

Filled with 'White' Color

Filled with 'Black' Color

Filled with 'Gray' Color

Filled with 'Dark Gray' Color

PATTERN COMPLETION

Fill Pattern

Triangle

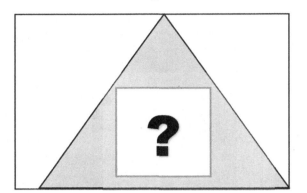

Triangle – one side intersecting with one corner of Square

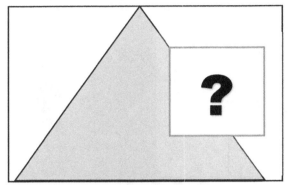

Triangle – one side intersecting with two corners of Square

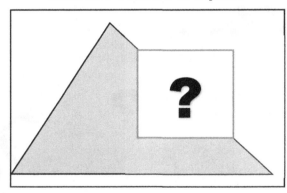

Triangle – Two sides intersecting with Square

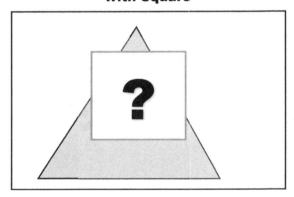

PATTERN COMPLETION
Fill Pattern

Circle in front of the Triangle

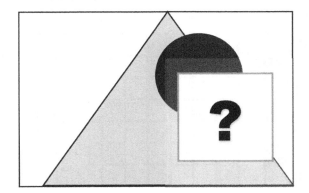

Circle behind the Triangle

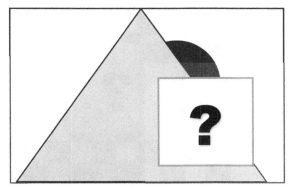

Gray stripes in front of Black Stripes

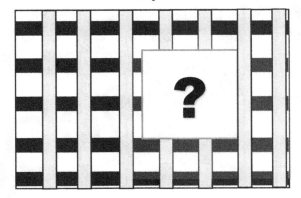

Gray stripes behind the Black Stripes

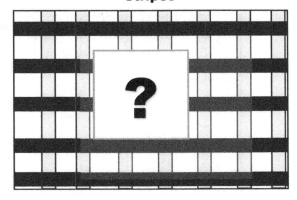

PATTERN COMPLETION
Fill Pattern

Grid Pattern – Alternating Black and White

Grid Pattern – 2 White, 1 Gray squares &

1 Gray, 2 White squares

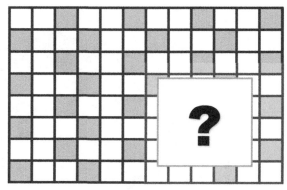

Grid Pattern – 3 White, 1 Gray squares &

1 Gray, 3 White squares

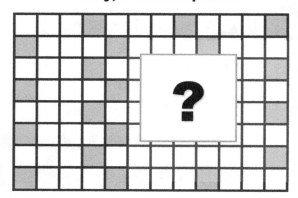

Grid Pattern – 1 White, 2 Black squares &

1 Black, 2 White squares

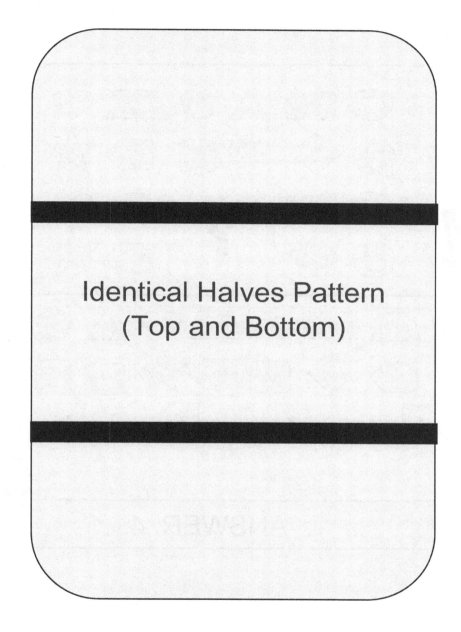

Identical Halves Pattern
(Top and Bottom)

PATTERN COMPLETION

Question

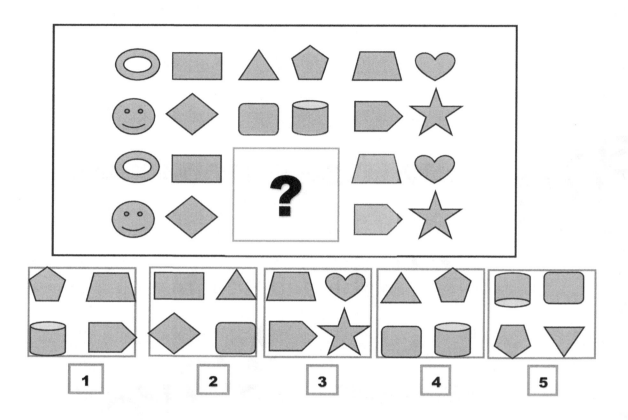

ANSWER: 4

16

PATTERN COMPLETION

HOW TO SOLVE?

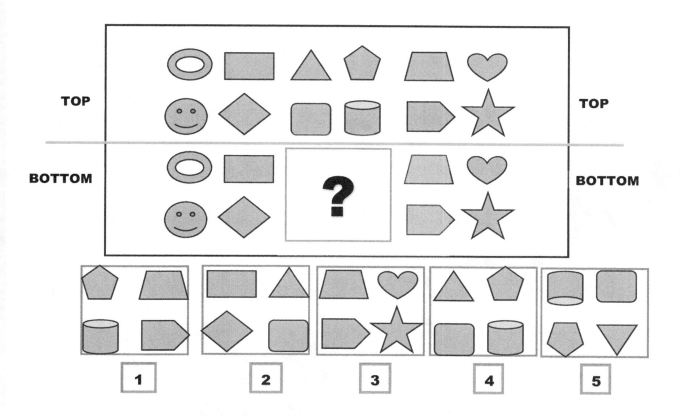

How to solve?

STEP-1: Understand given pattern. **Top two rows are IDENTICAL to bottom two rows.**

STEP-2: Complete the pattern

STEP-3: Find the correct Answer

ANSWER is 4

17

PATTERN COMPLETION

HOW TO SOLVE?

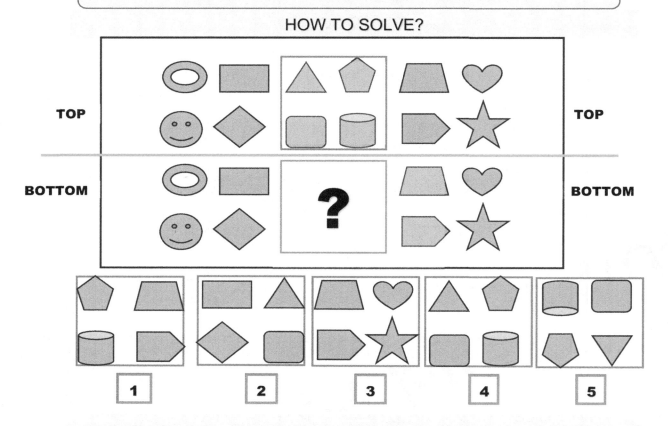

How to solve?

STEP-1: Understand given pattern. **Top two rows are IDENTICAL to bottom two rows.**

STEP-2: Complete the pattern

STEP-3: Find the correct Answer

ANSWER is 4

Answer 1 is incorrect. Shapes DO NOT Match.

Answer 2 is incorrect. Shapes DO NOT Match.

Answer 3 is incorrect. Shapes DO NOT Match.

Answer 5 is incorrect. Shapes DO NOT Match.

PATTERN COMPLETION

Identical Halves Pattern

TOP

TOP

BOTTOM

BOTTOM

Top 3 rows are IDENTICAL to bottom 3 rows.

PATTERN COMPLETION

Identical Halves Pattern

Top 3 rows are IDENTICAL to bottom 3 rows.

PATTERN COMPLETION

Identical Halves Pattern

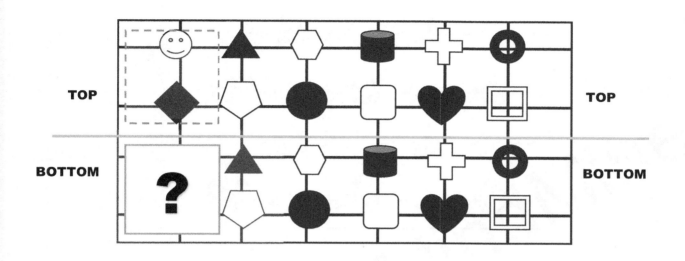

TOP

BOTTOM

TOP

BOTTOM

Top 2 rows are IDENTICAL to bottom 2 rows.

PATTERN COMPLETION

Identical Halves Pattern

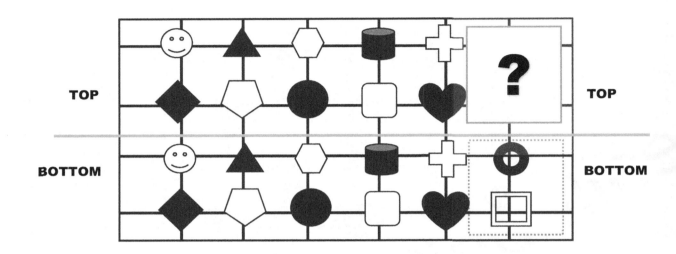

Bottom 2 rows are IDENTICAL to Top 2 rows.

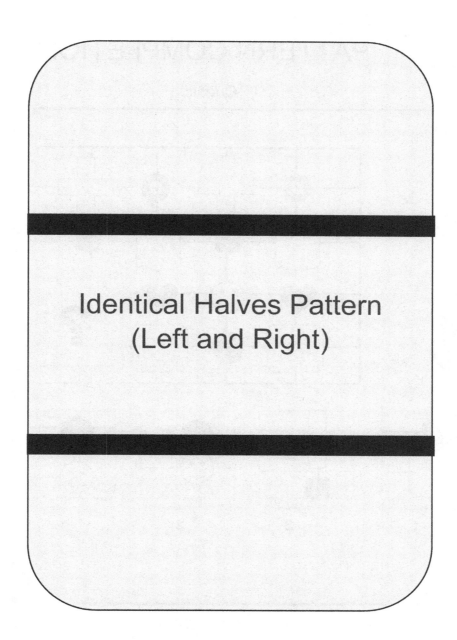

Identical Halves Pattern
(Left and Right)

PATTERN COMPLETION

Question

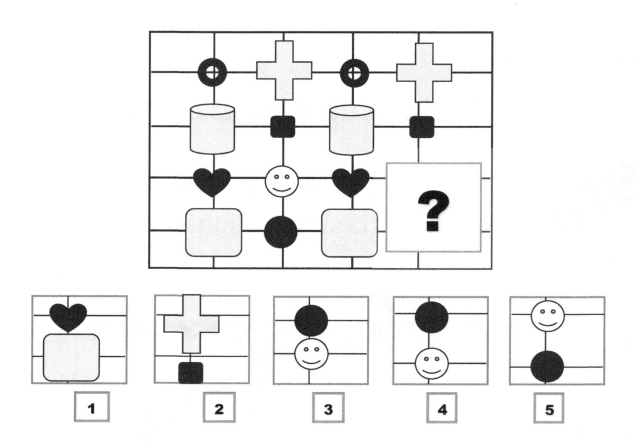

| 1 | 2 | 3 | 4 | 5 |

ANSWER: 5

PATTERN COMPLETION

HOW TO SOLVE?

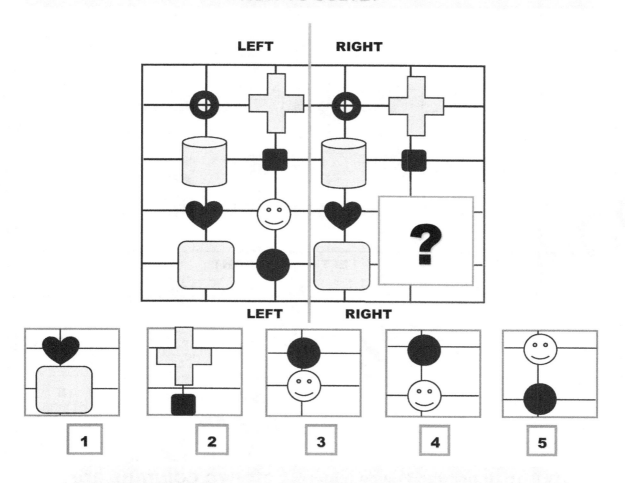

How to solve?

STEP-1: Understand given pattern. **Left two columns are IDENTICAL to Right two columns.**

STEP-2: Complete the pattern

STEP-3: Find the correct Answer

ANSWER is 5

PATTERN COMPLETION

HOW TO SOLVE?

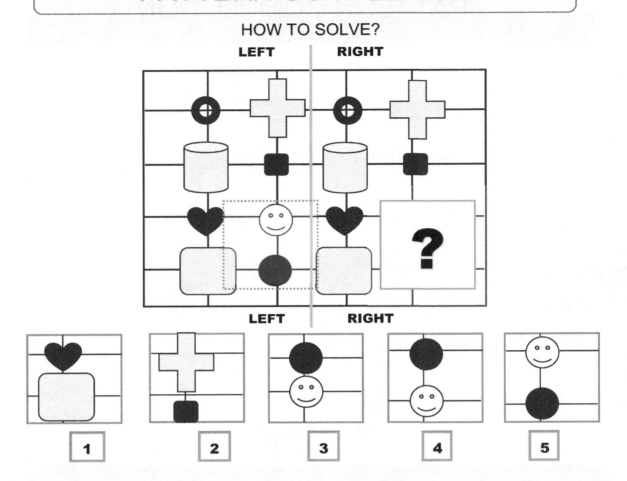

How to solve?

STEP-1: Understand given pattern. **Left two columns are IDENTICAL to Right two columns.**

STEP-2: Complete the pattern

STEP-3: Find the correct Answer

ANSWER is 5

Answer 1 is incorrect. Shapes DO NOT Match.

Answer 2 is incorrect. Shapes DO NOT Match.

Answer 3 is incorrect. Shapes DO NOT Match.

Answer 4 is incorrect. Shapes DO NOT Match.

PATTERN COMPLETION

Identical Halves Pattern

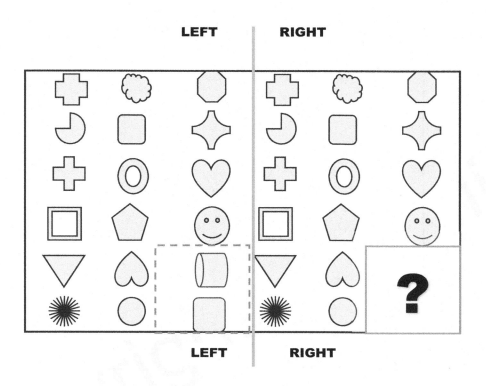

Left 3 columns are IDENTICAL to

Right 3 columns.

PATTERN COMPLETION

Identical Halves Pattern

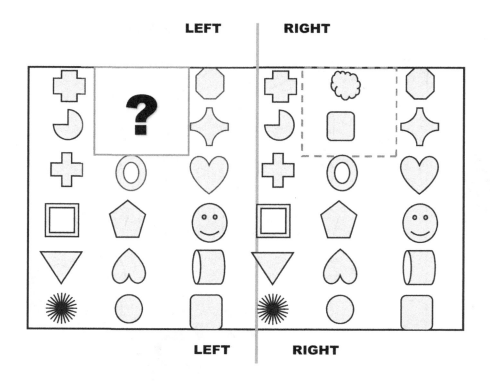

Right 3 columns are IDENTICAL to

Left 3 columns.

PATTERN COMPLETION

Identical Halves Pattern

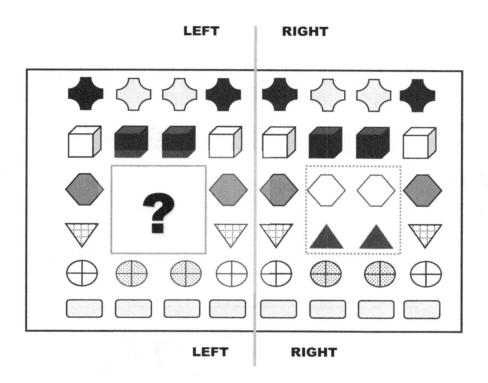

Right 4 columns are IDENTICAL to

Left 4 columns.

PATTERN COMPLETION

Identical Halves Pattern

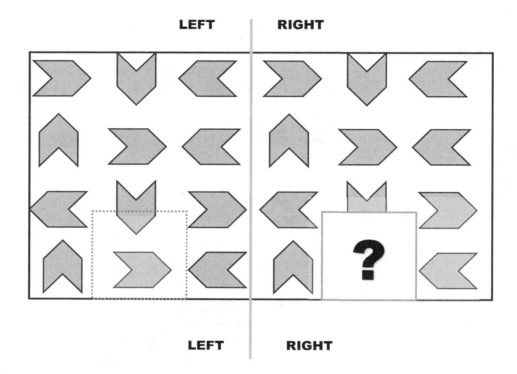

Left 3 columns are IDENTICAL to

Right 3 columns.

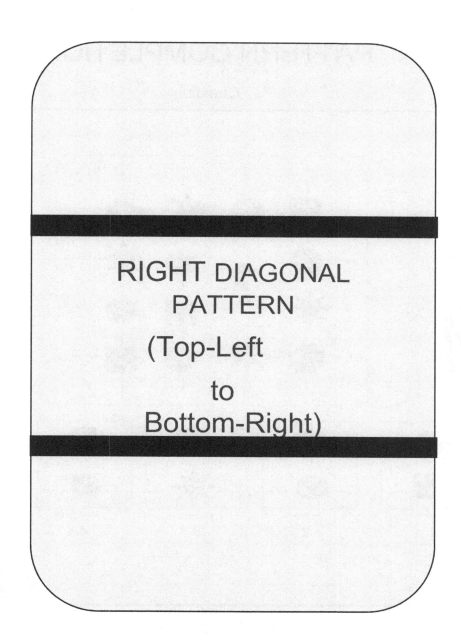

RIGHT DIAGONAL
PATTERN
(Top-Left
to
Bottom-Right)

PATTERN COMPLETION

Question

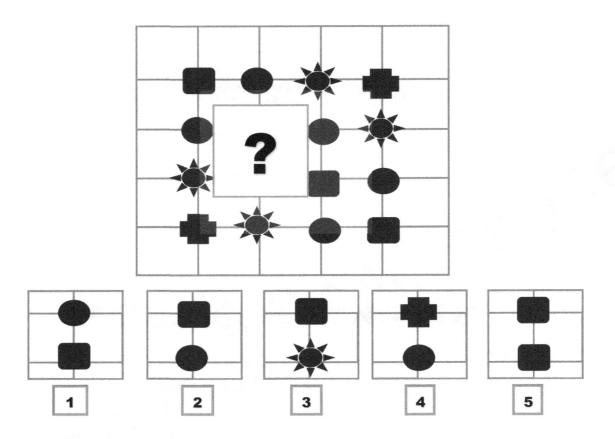

1 2 3 4 5

ANSWER: 2

32

PATTERN COMPLETION

HOW TO SOLVE?

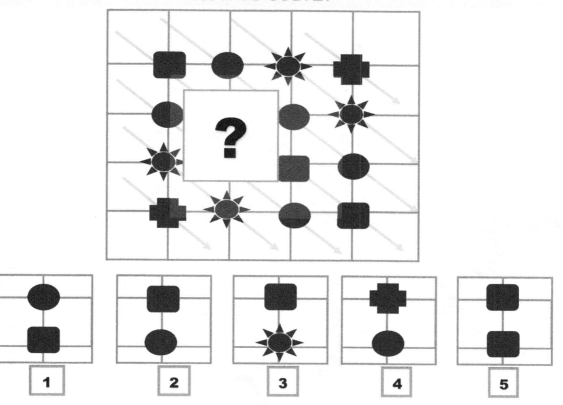

How to solve?

STEP-1: Understand given pattern. Figures are same in **Top-Left to Bottom-Right (Right Diagonal)** direction.

STEP-2: Complete the pattern

STEP-3: Find the correct Answer

ANSWER is 2

PATTERN COMPLETION

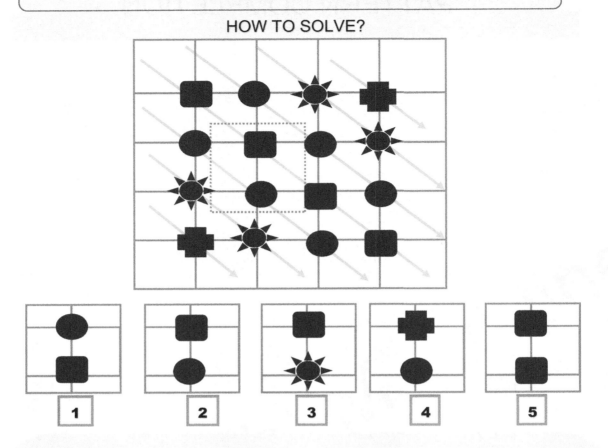

How to solve?

STEP-1: Understand given pattern. Figures are same in **Top-Left to Bottom-Right (Right Diagonal)** direction.

STEP-2: Complete the pattern

STEP-3: Find the correct Answer

ANSWER is 2

Answer 1 is incorrect. Shapes DO NOT Match.

Answer 3 is incorrect. Shapes DO NOT Match.

Answer 4 is incorrect. Shapes DO NOT Match.

Answer 5 is incorrect. Shapes DO NOT Match.

PATTERN COMPLETION

HOW TO SOLVE?

Figures are same in **Top-Left to Bottom-Right (Right Diagonal)** direction.

35

PATTERN COMPLETION

HOW TO SOLVE?

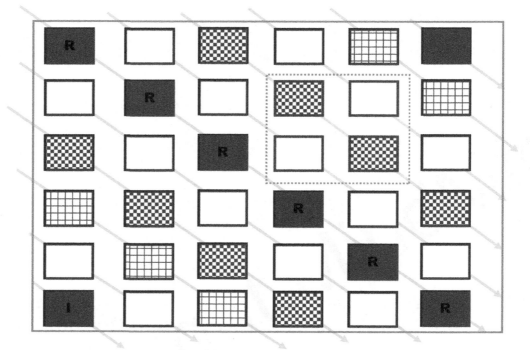

Figures are same in **Top-Left to Bottom-Right (Right Diagonal)** direction.

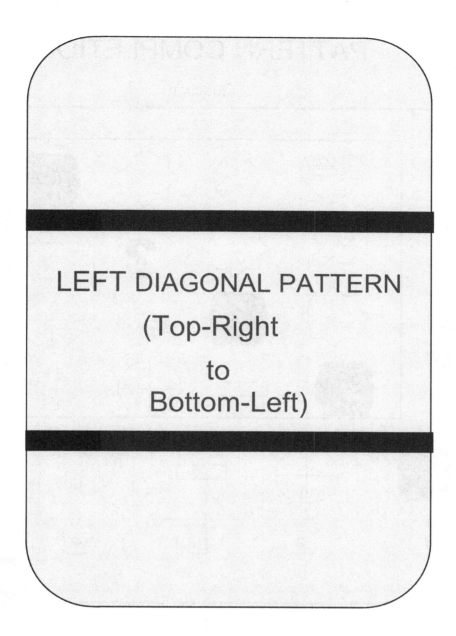

LEFT DIAGONAL PATTERN
(Top-Right
to
Bottom-Left)

PATTERN COMPLETION

Question

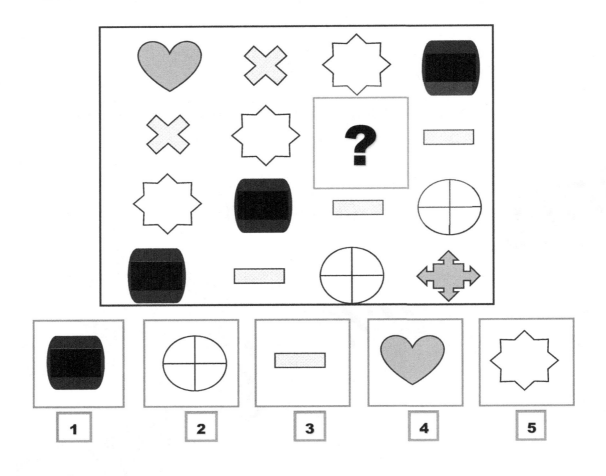

ANSWER: 1

PATTERN COMPLETION

HOW TO SOLVE?

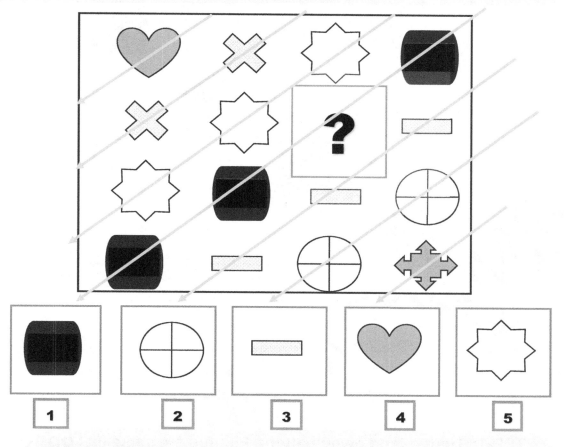

How to solve?

STEP-1: Understand given pattern. Figures are same in **Top-Right to Bottom-Left (Left Diagonal)** direction.

STEP-2: Complete the pattern

STEP-3: Find the correct Answer

ANSWER is 1

PATTERN COMPLETION

HOW TO SOLVE?

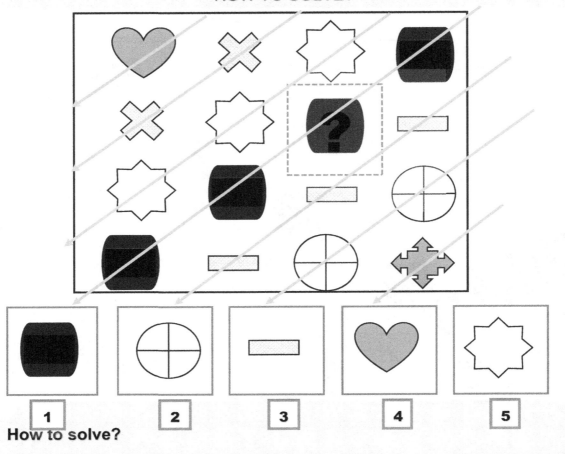

How to solve?

STEP-1: Understand given pattern. Figures are same in **Top-Right to Bottom-Left (Left Diagonal)** direction.

STEP-2: Complete the pattern

STEP-3: Find the correct Answer

ANSWER is 1

Answer 2 is incorrect. Shapes DO NOT Match.

Answer 3 is incorrect. Shapes DO NOT Match.

Answer 4 is incorrect. Shapes DO NOT Match.

Answer 5 is incorrect. Shapes DO NOT Match.

PATTERN COMPLETION

HOW TO SOLVE?

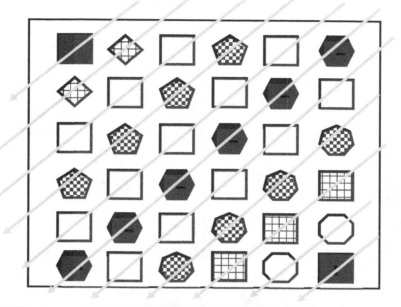

Figures are same in **Top-Right to Bottom-Left (Left Diagonal)** direction

PATTERN COMPLETION

HOW TO SOLVE?

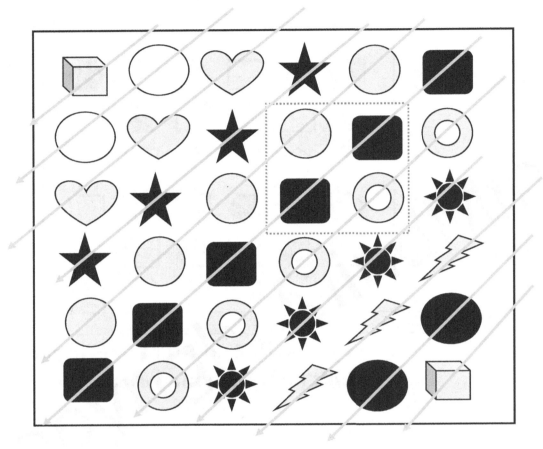

Figures are same in Top-Right to Bottom-Left (Left Diagonal) direction

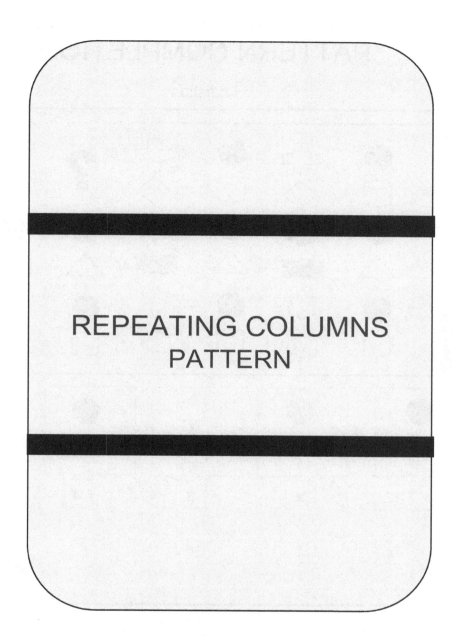

REPEATING COLUMNS
PATTERN

PATTERN COMPLETION

Question

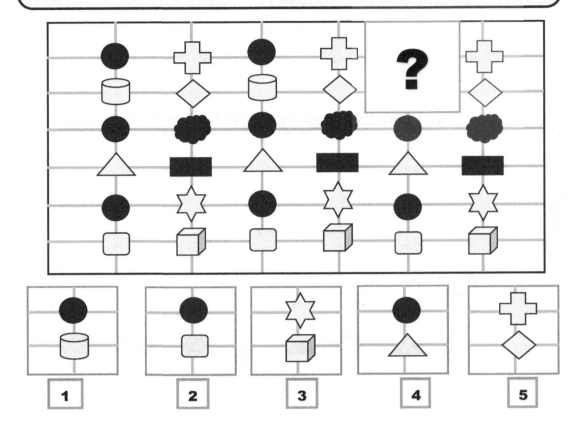

| 1 | 2 | 3 | 4 | 5 |

ANSWER: 1

44

PATTERN COMPLETION

HOW TO SOLVE?

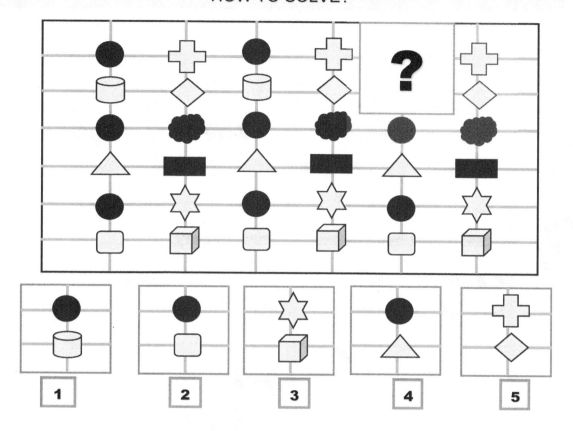

1 **2** **3** **4** **5**

How to solve?

STEP-1: Understand given pattern. Two columns are Repeating

STEP-2: Complete the pattern

STEP-3: Find the correct Answer

ANSWER is 1

PATTERN COMPLETION

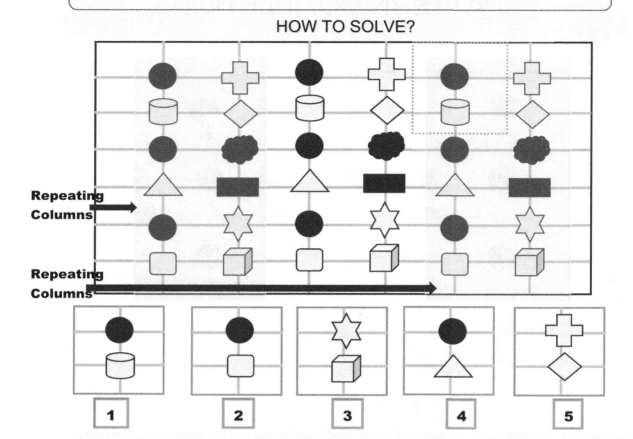

How to solve?

STEP-1: Understand given pattern. Two columns are Repeating

STEP-2: Complete the pattern

STEP-3: Find the correct Answer

ANSWER is 1

Answer 2 is incorrect. Shapes DO NOT Match.

Answer 3 is incorrect. Shapes DO NOT Match.

Answer 4 is incorrect. Shapes DO NOT Match.

Answer 5 is incorrect. Shapes DO NOT Match.

PATTERN COMPLETION

HOW TO SOLVE?

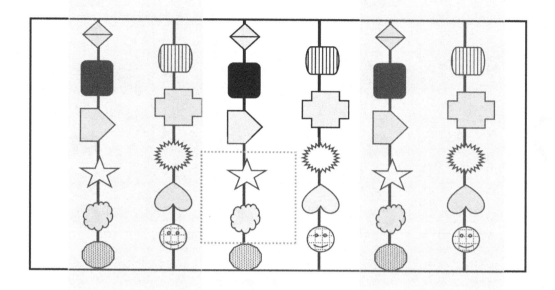

Repeating Columns

PATTERN COMPLETION

HOW TO SOLVE?

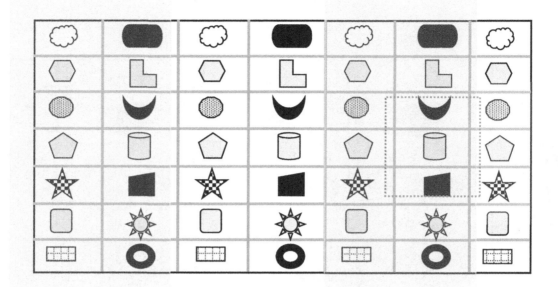

Repeating Columns

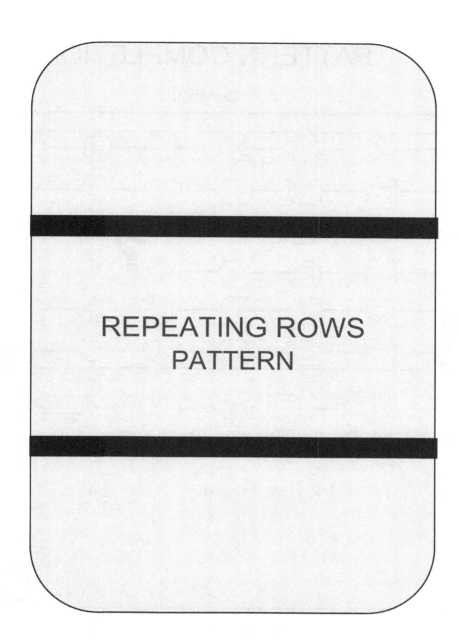

REPEATING ROWS
PATTERN

PATTERN COMPLETION

Question

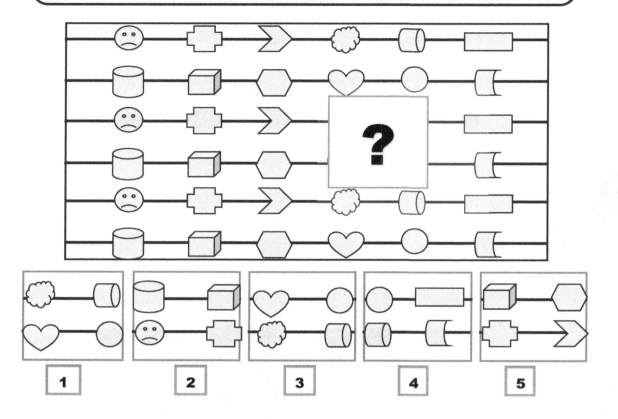

ANSWER: 1

PATTERN COMPLETION

HOW TO SOLVE?

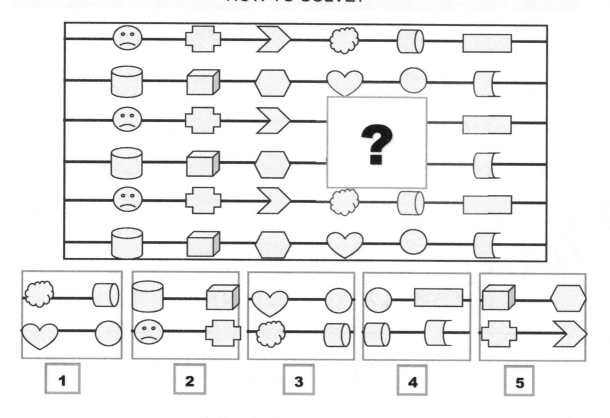

How to solve?

STEP-1: Understand given pattern. Two Rows are Repeating

STEP-2: Complete the pattern

STEP-3: Find the correct Answer

ANSWER is 1

PATTERN COMPLETION

HOW TO SOLVE?

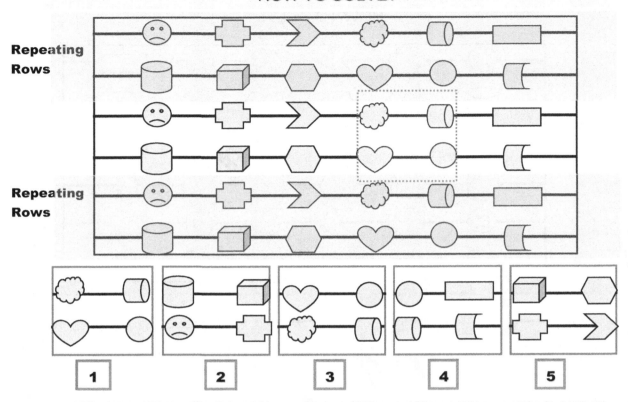

Repeating Rows

Repeating Rows

How to solve?

STEP-1: Understand given pattern. Two columns are Repeating

STEP-2: Complete the pattern

STEP-3: Find the correct Answer

ANSWER is 1

Answer 2 is incorrect. Shapes DO NOT Match.

Answer 3 is incorrect. Shapes DO NOT Match.

Answer 4 is incorrect. Shapes DO NOT Match.

Answer 5 is incorrect. Shapes DO NOT Match.

PATTERN COMPLETION

HOW TO SOLVE?

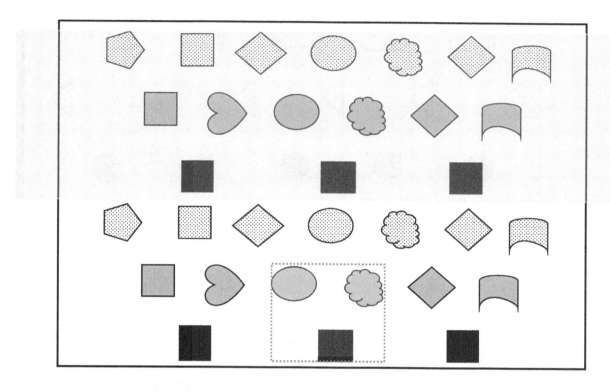

Repeating Rows

PATTERN COMPLETION

HOW TO SOLVE?

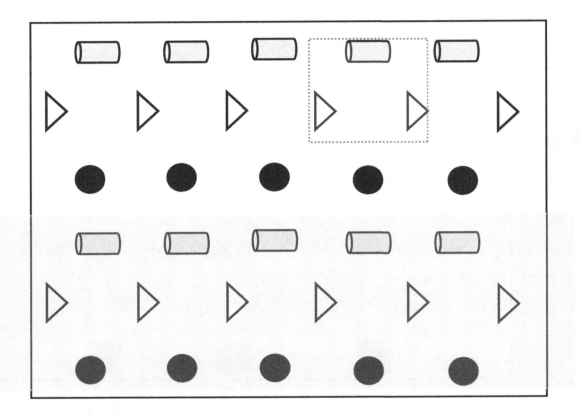

Repeating Rows

GIFTED & TALENTED

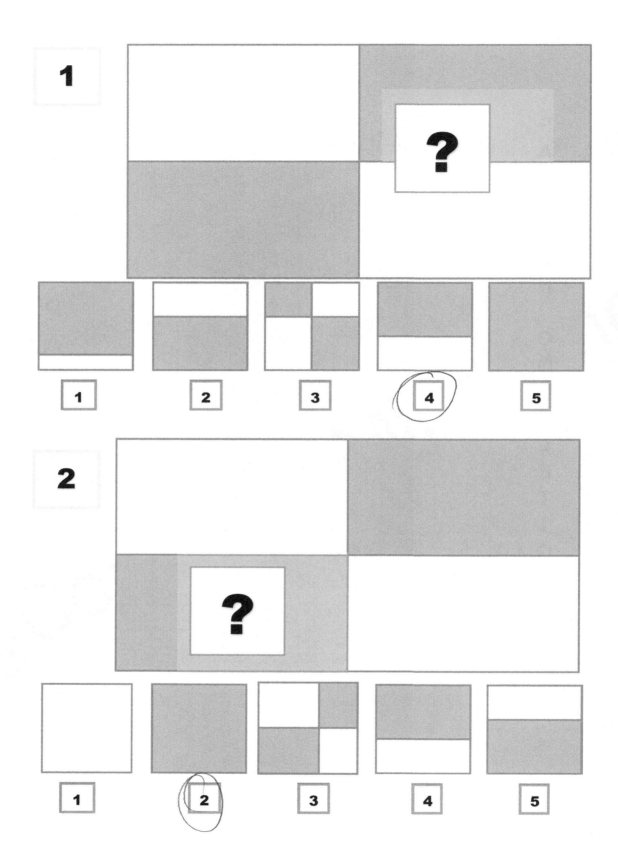

58

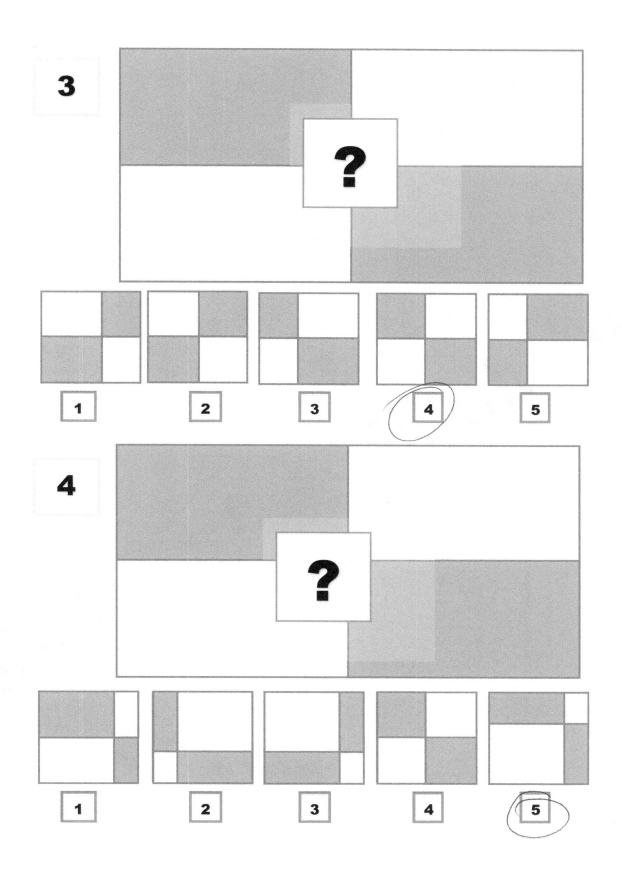

59

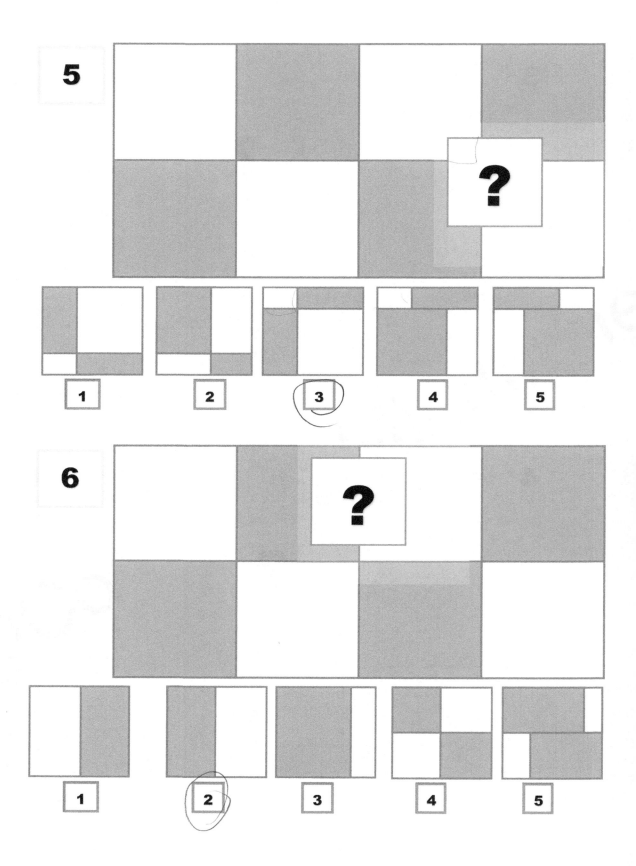

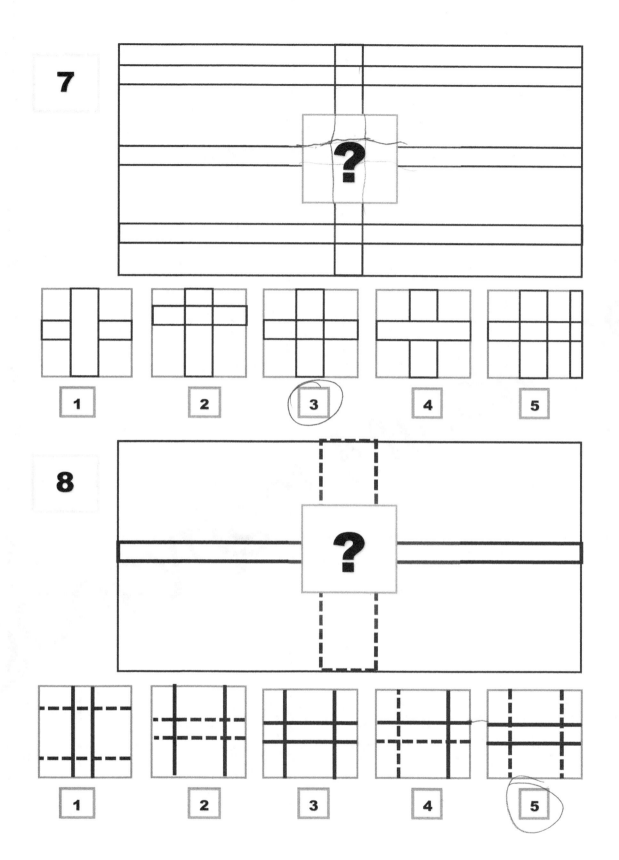

7

1 2 3 4 5

8

1 2 3 4 5

61

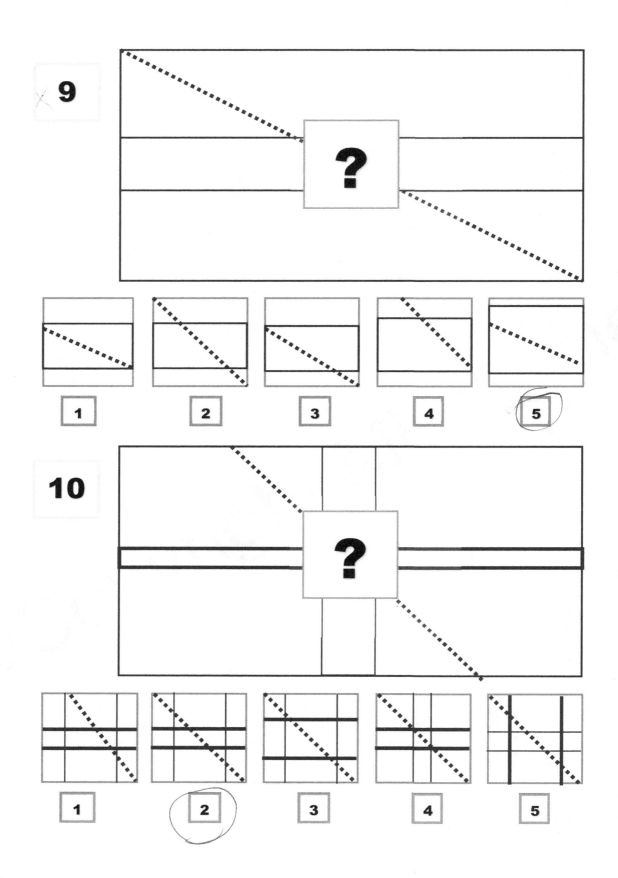

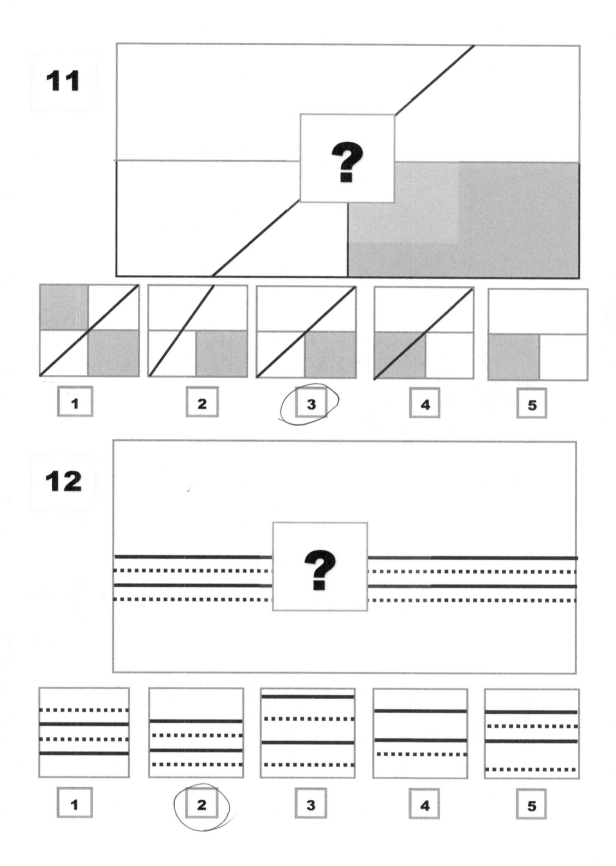

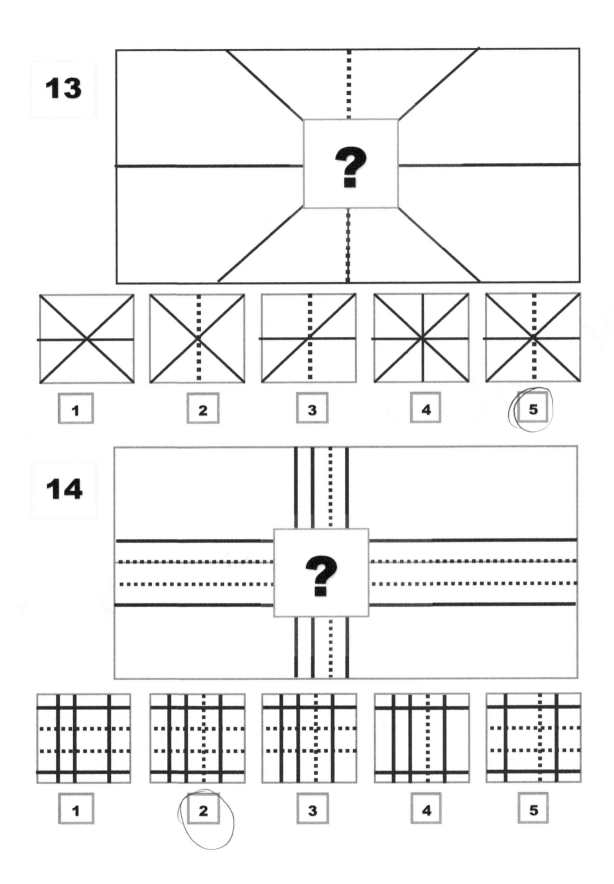

13

1 2 3 4 **5**

14

1 **2** 3 4 5

64

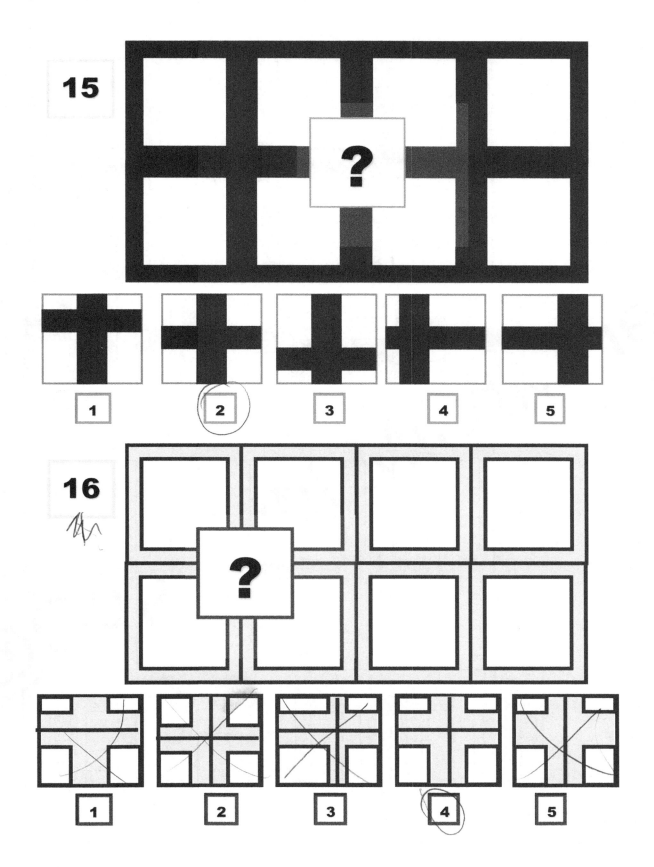

15

1 2 3 4 5

16

1 2 3 4 5

65

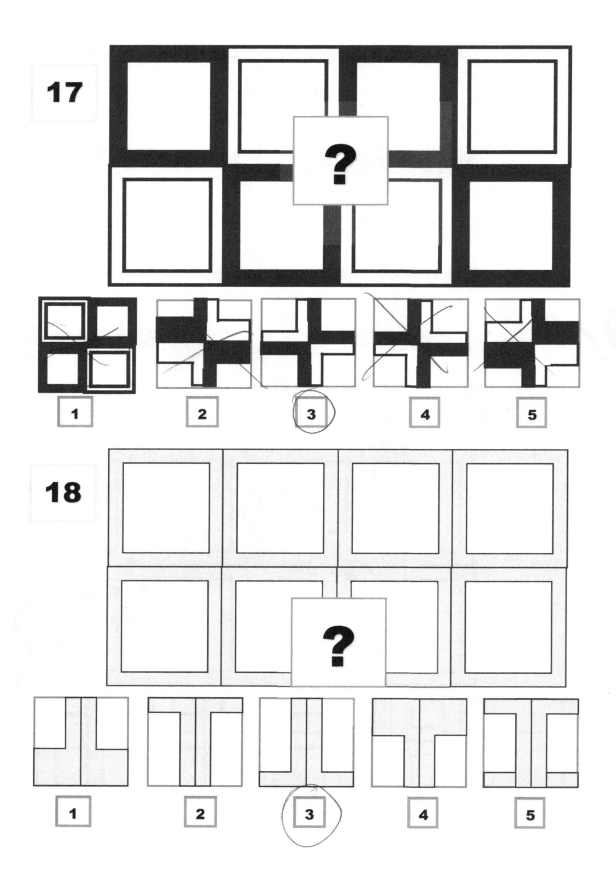

17

1   2   3   4   5

18

1   2   3   4   5

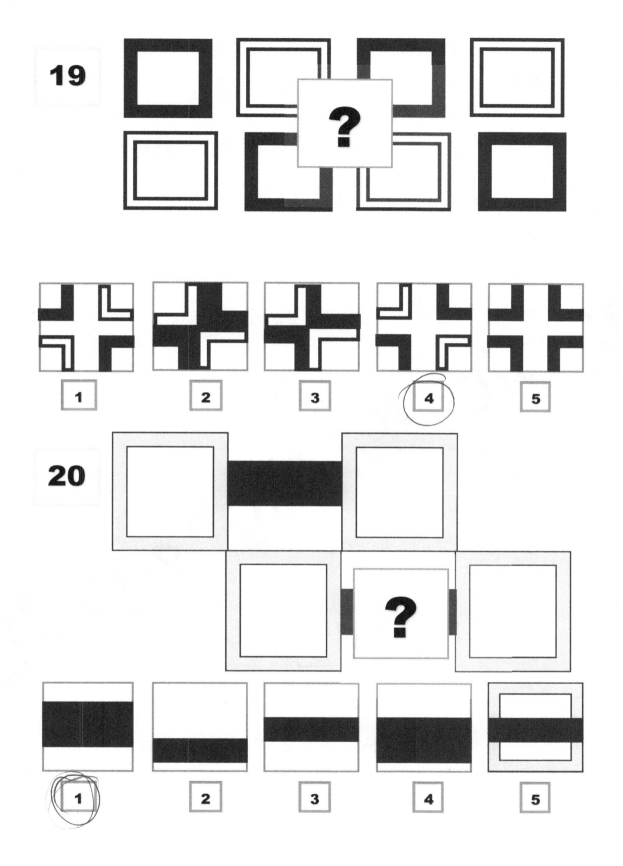

19

20

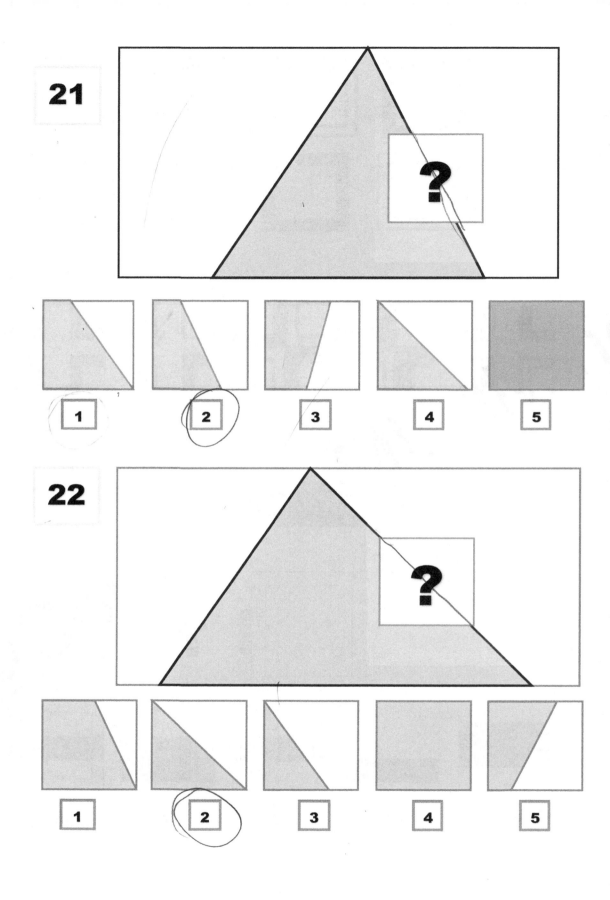

68

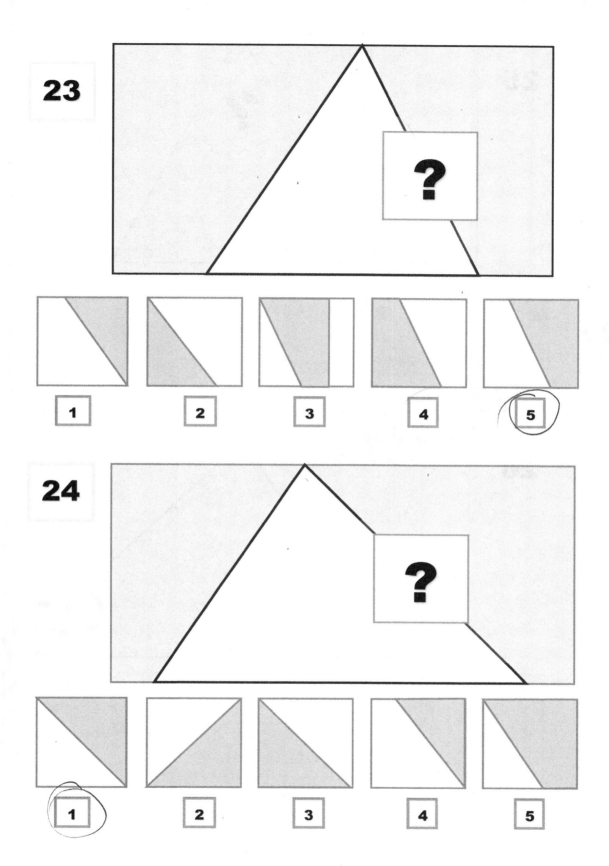

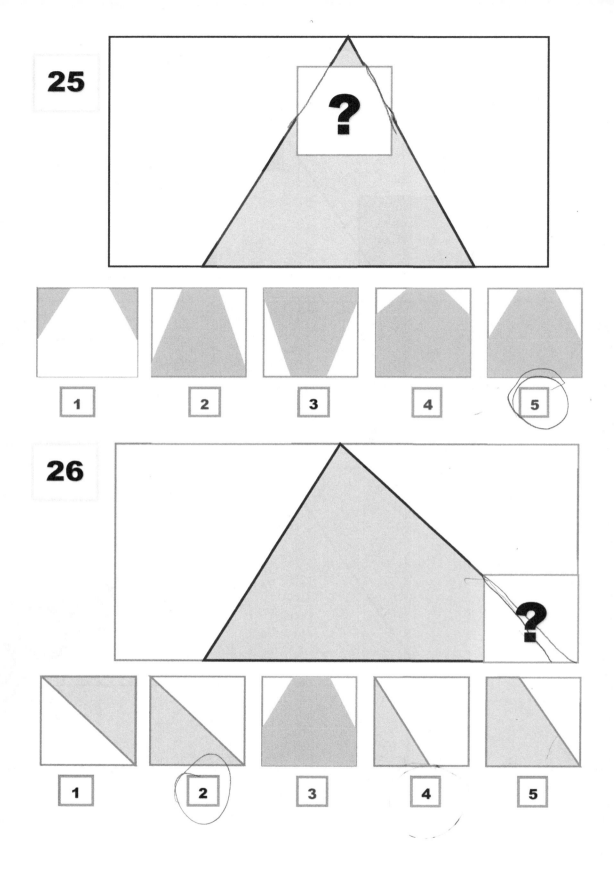

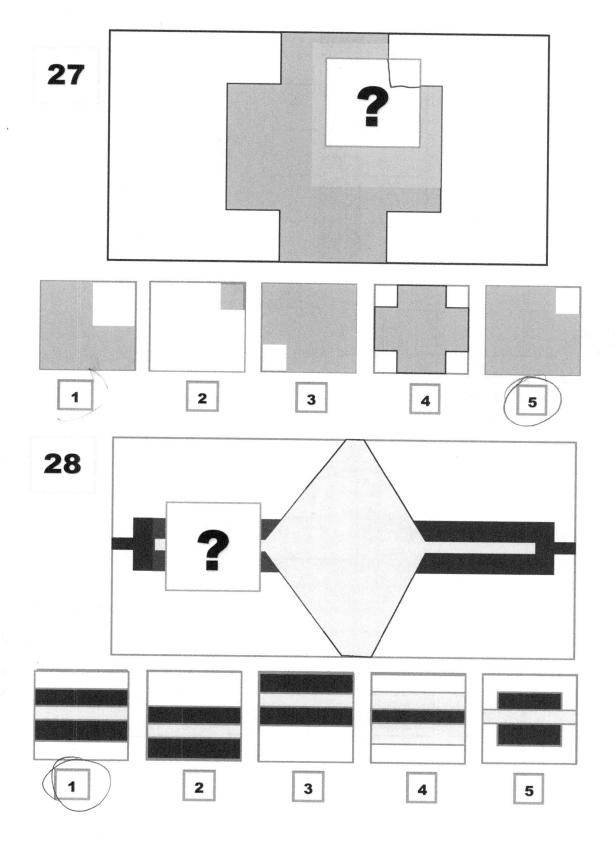

27

28

29

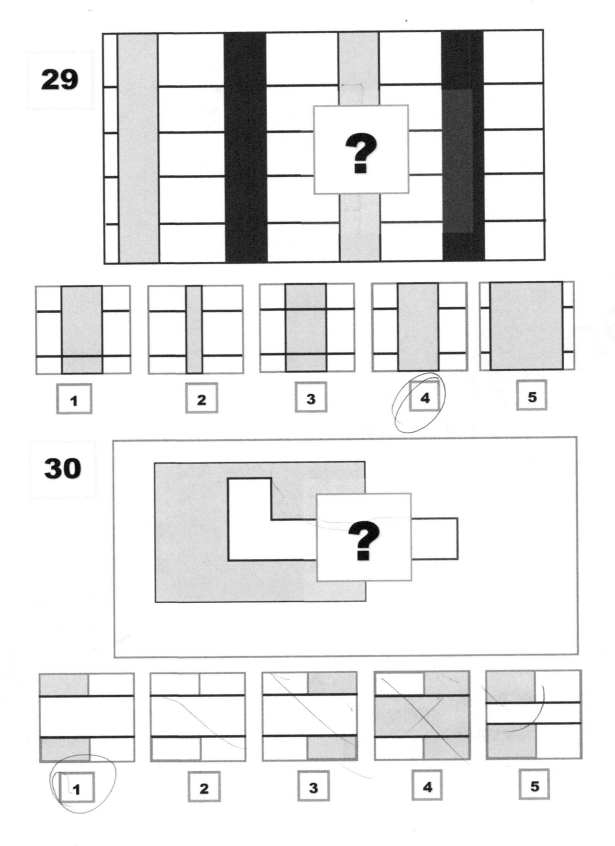

1   **2**   **3**   **4**   **5**

30

1   **2**   **3**   **4**   **5**

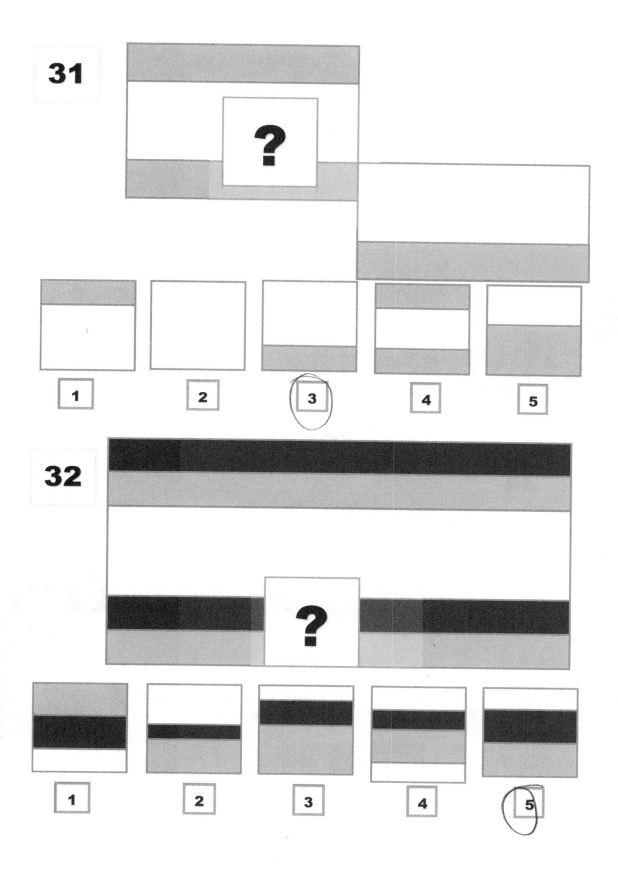

31

1 2 3 4 5

32

1 2 3 4 5

73

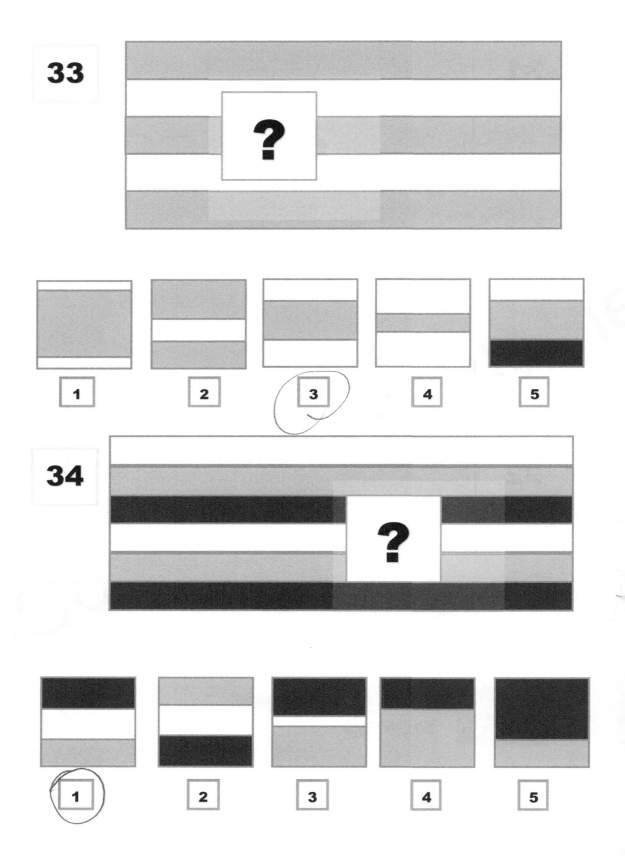

33

1 2 3 4 5

34

1 2 3 4 5

74

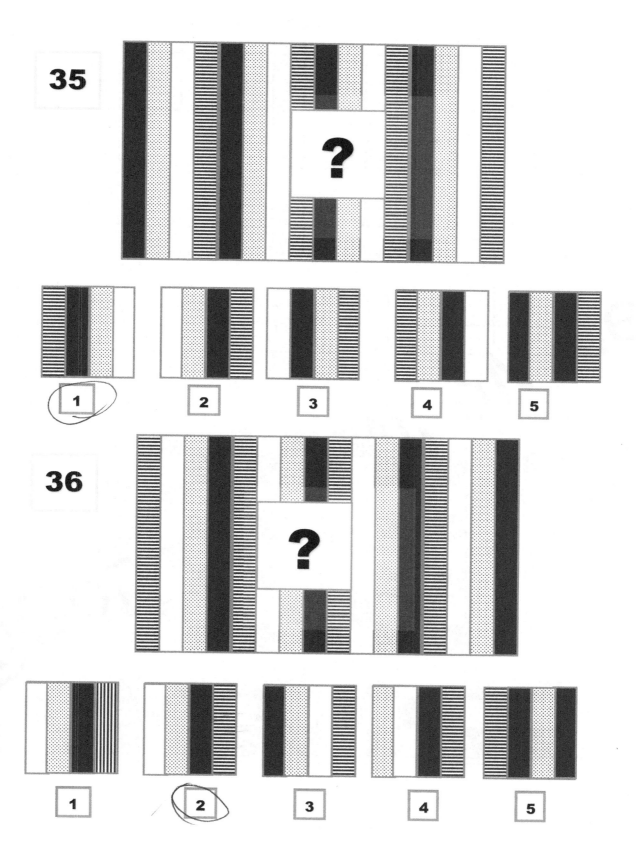

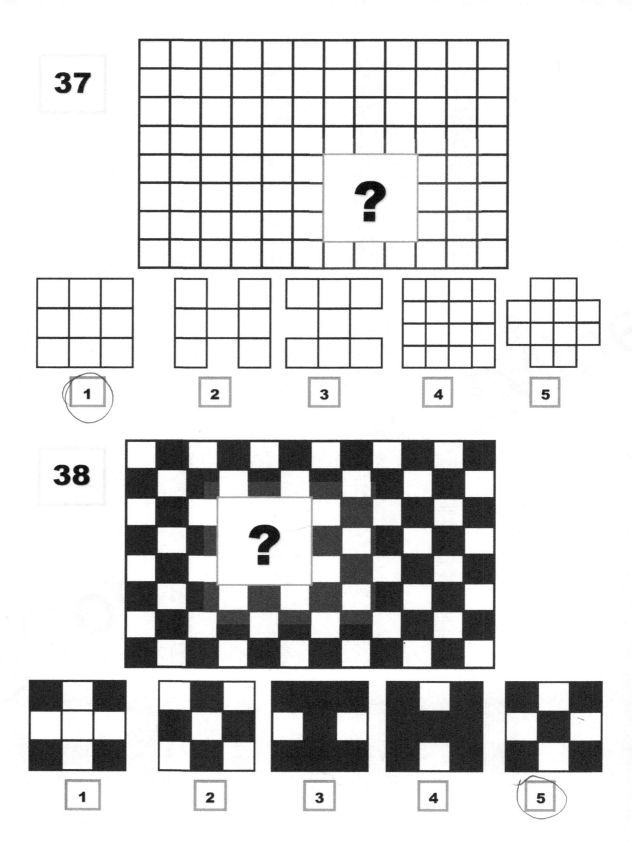

37

38

39

40

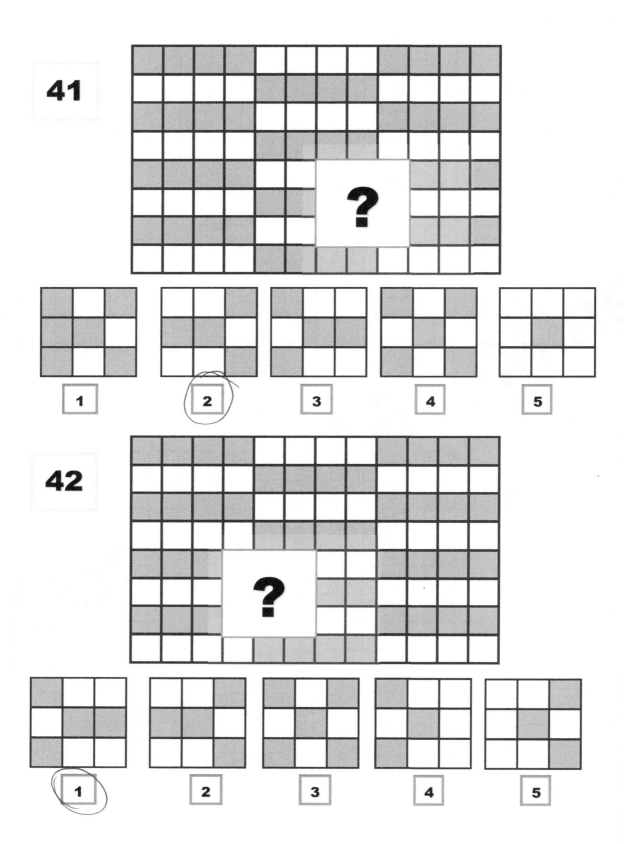

43

1   2   3   4   (5)

44

1   2   (3)   4   5

79

45

1 2 3 4 5

46

1 2 3 4 5

80

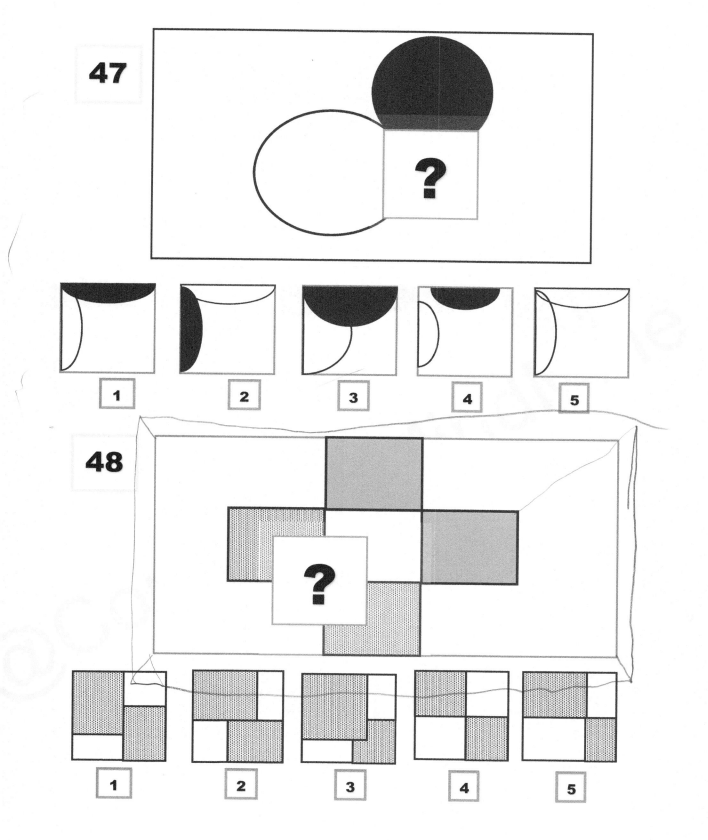

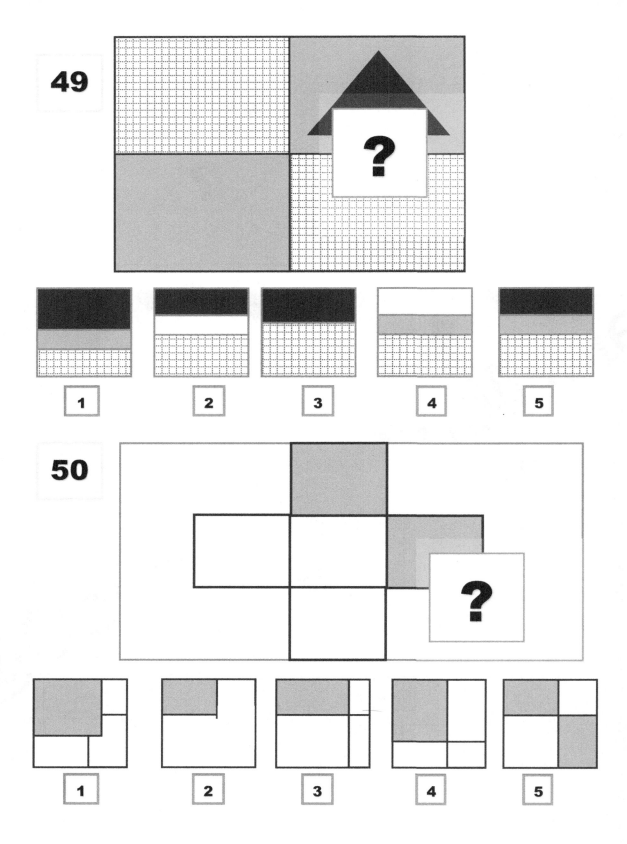

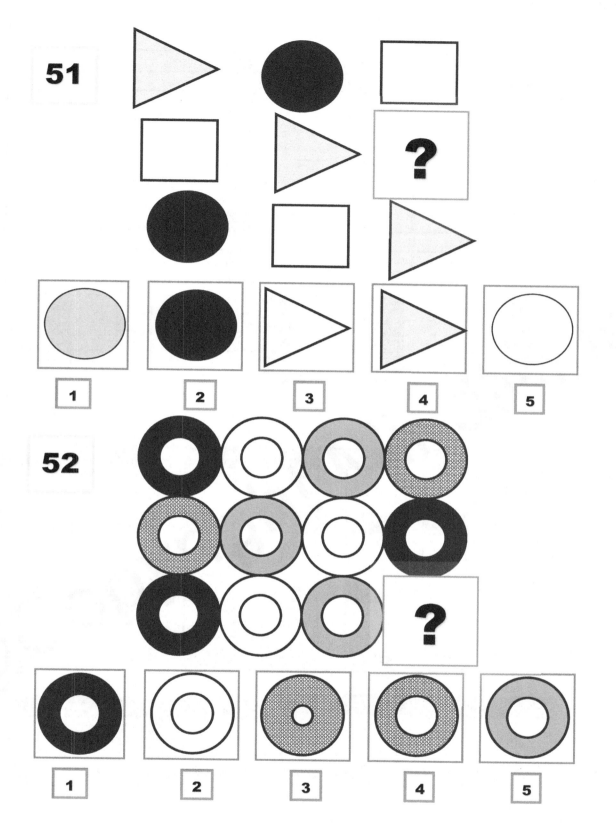

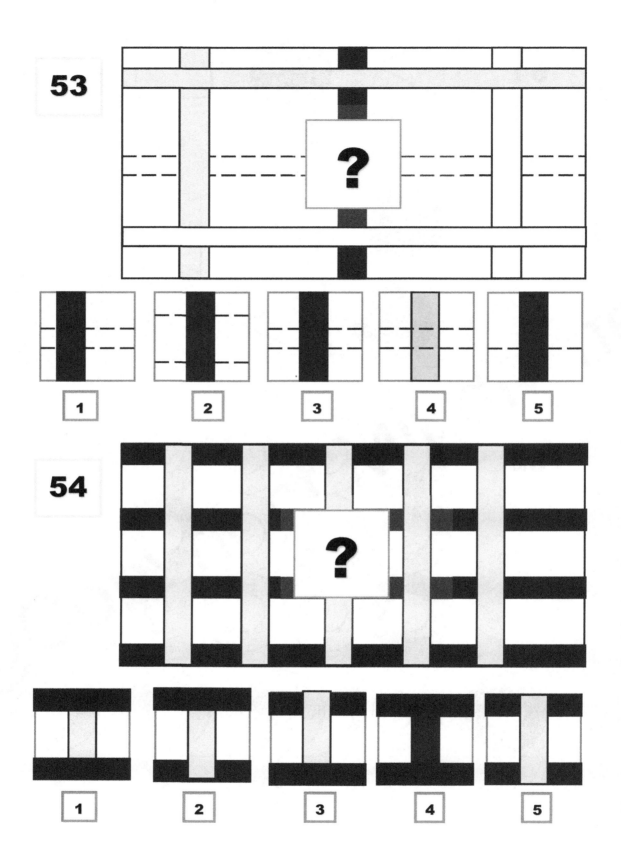

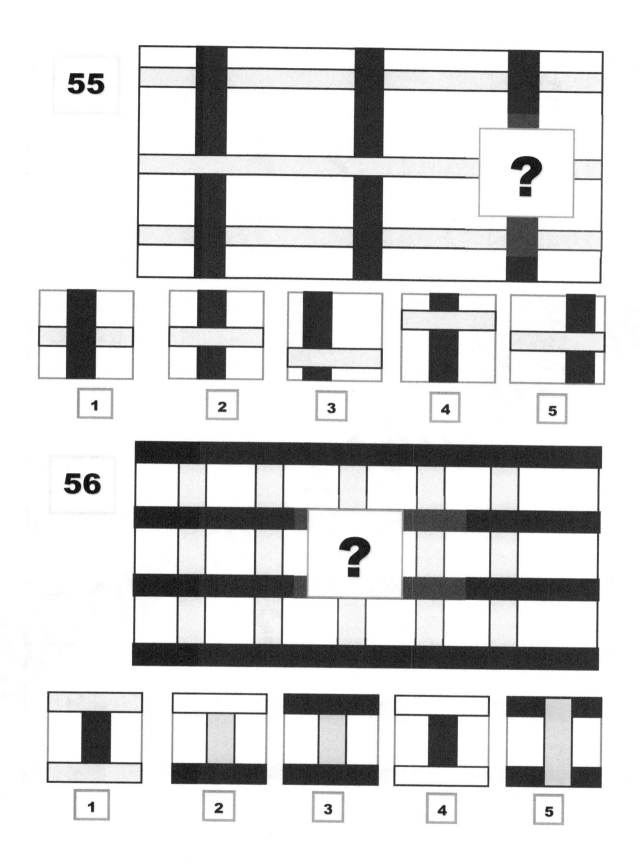

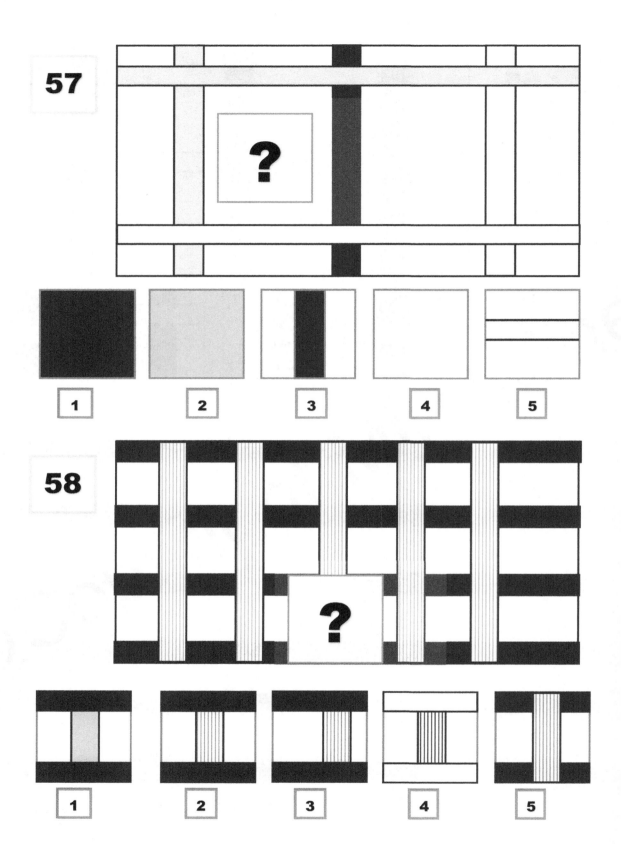

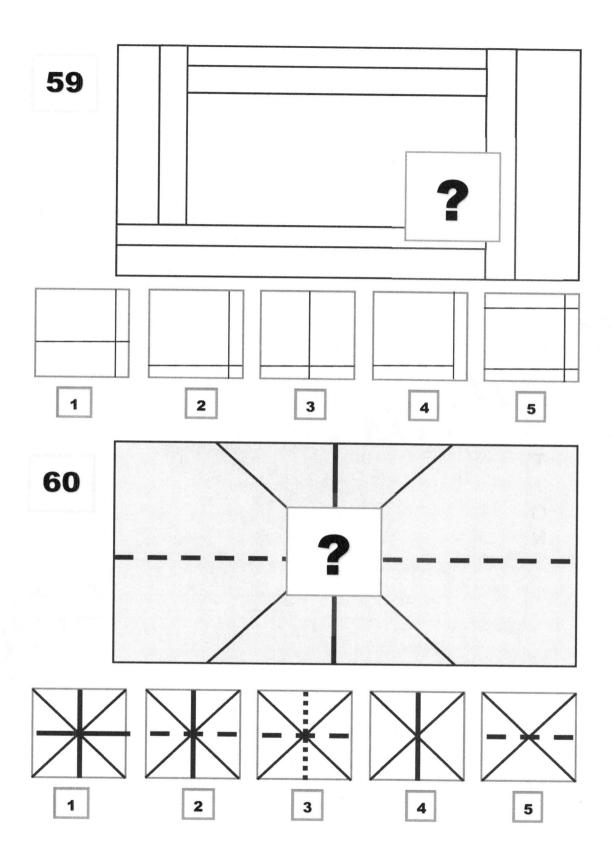

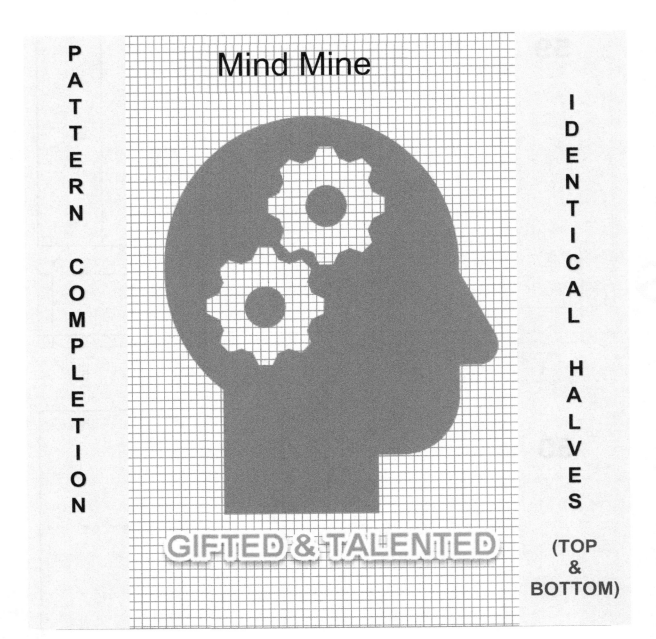

PATTERN COMPLETION

IDENTICAL HALVES

(TOP & BOTTOM)

GIFTED & TALENTED

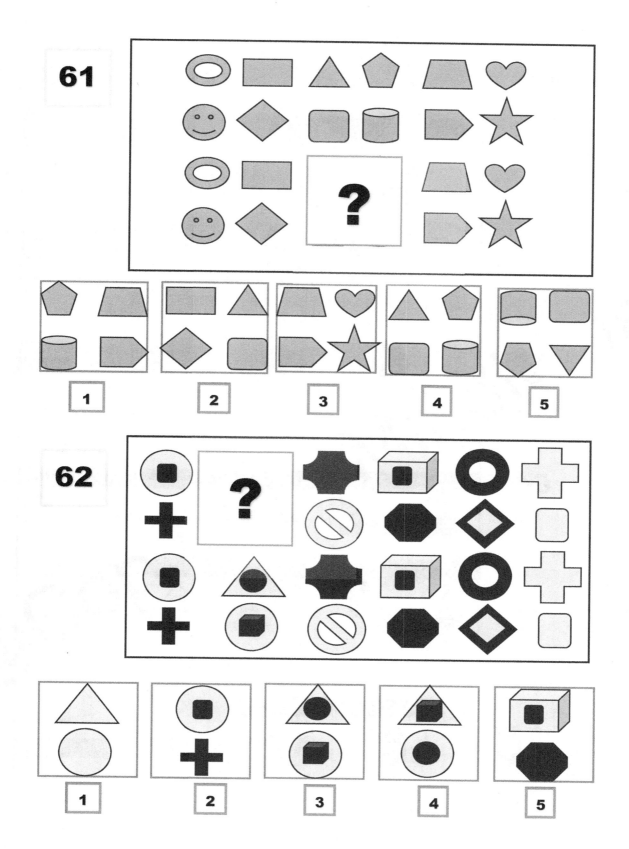

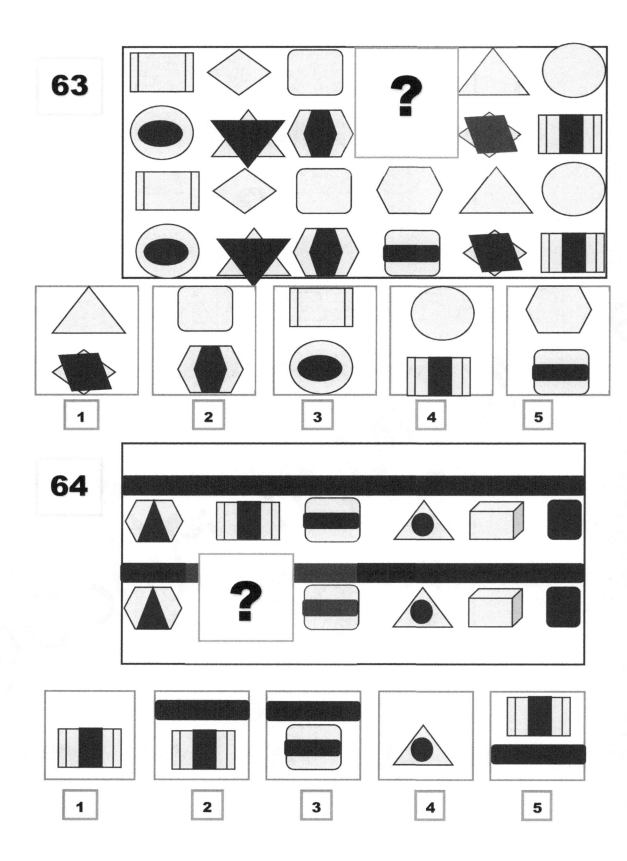

63

64

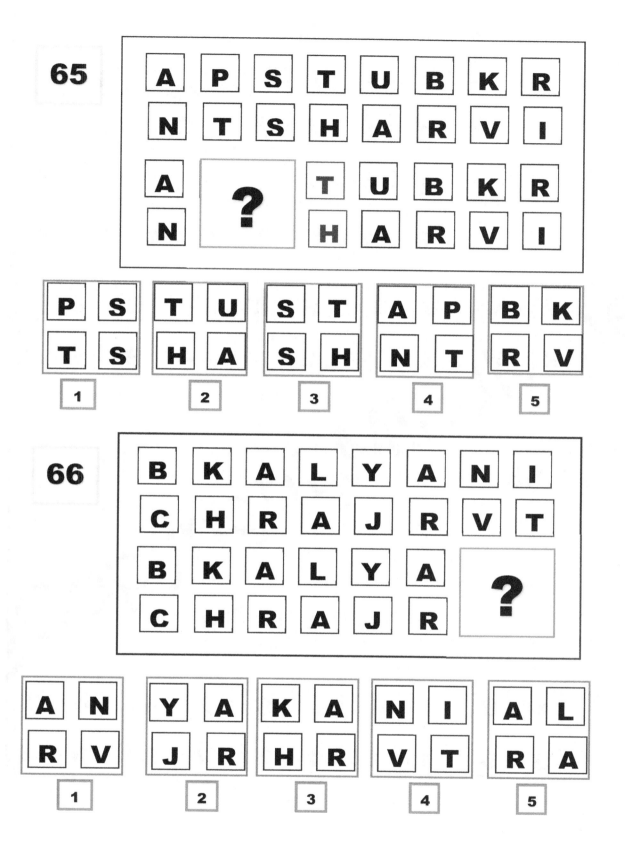

67

2	5	V	3	**?**		G	6
C	1	X	7			P	8
2	5	V	3	9	T	G	6
C	1	X	7	5	4	P	8

1	2	3	4	5
V 3 / X 7	V 3 / X 7	9 T / 5 4	T G / 4 P	G 6 / P 8

68

1	**?**		4	3	2	5	9
3			1	9	7	8	2
1	8	7	4	3	2	5	9
3	6	4	1	9	7	8	2

1	2	3	4	5
1 8 / 3 6	7 4 / 4 1	1 9 / 4 3	2 5 / 7 8	8 7 / 6 4

92

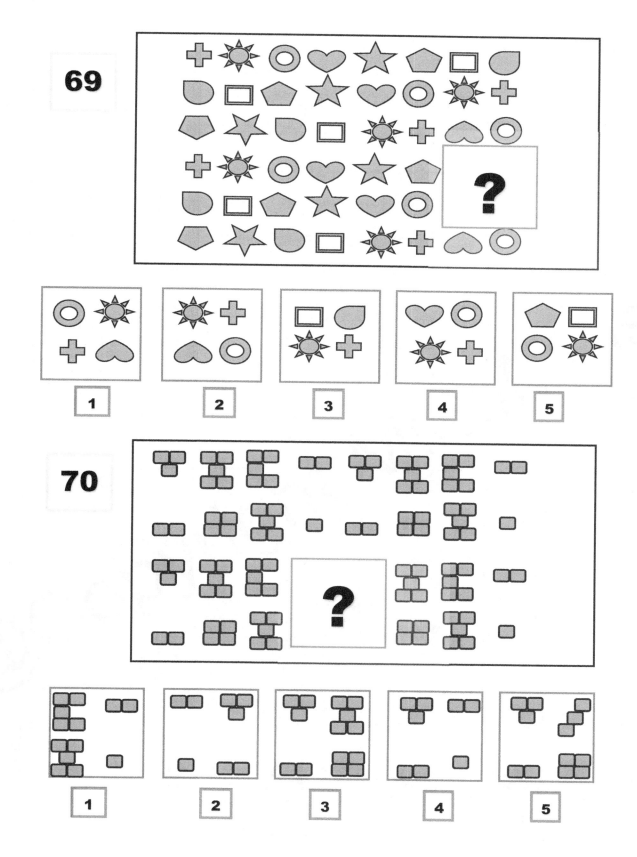

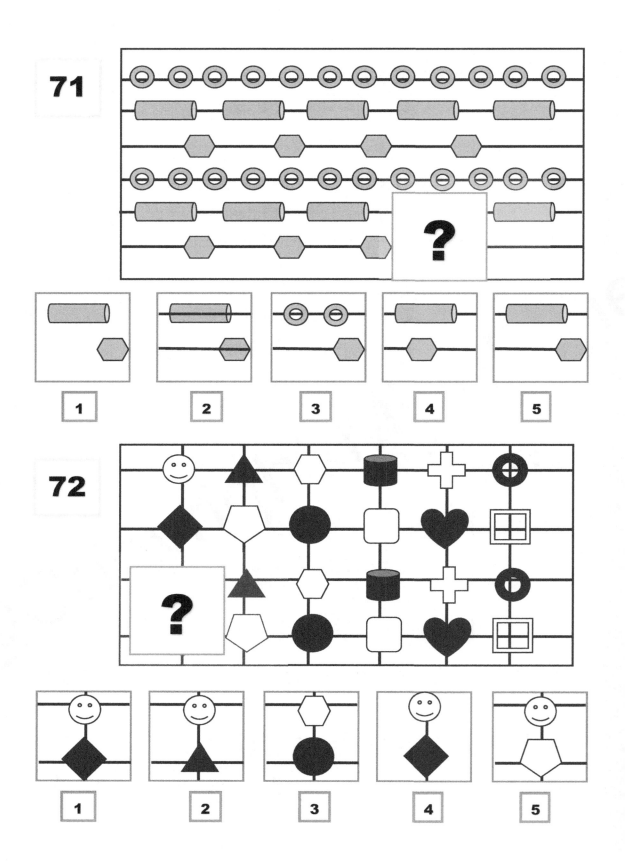

94

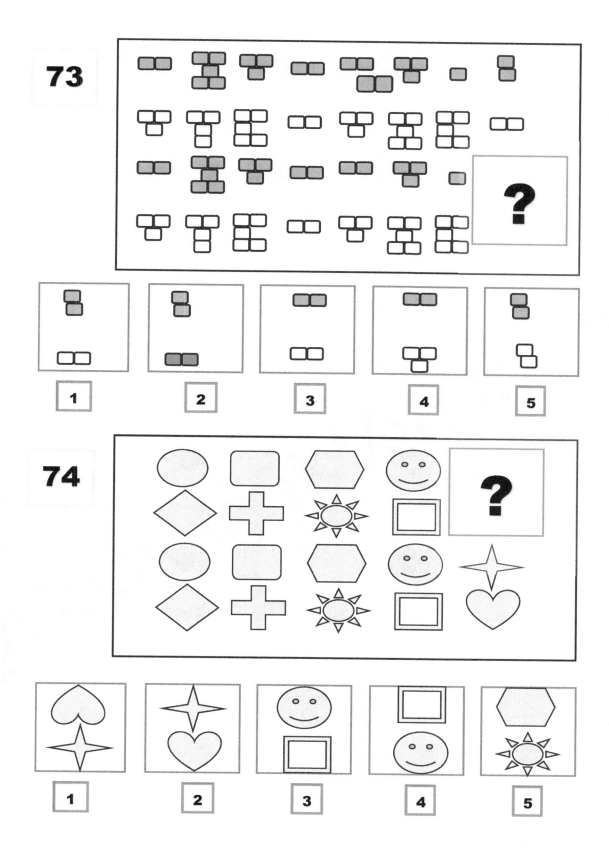

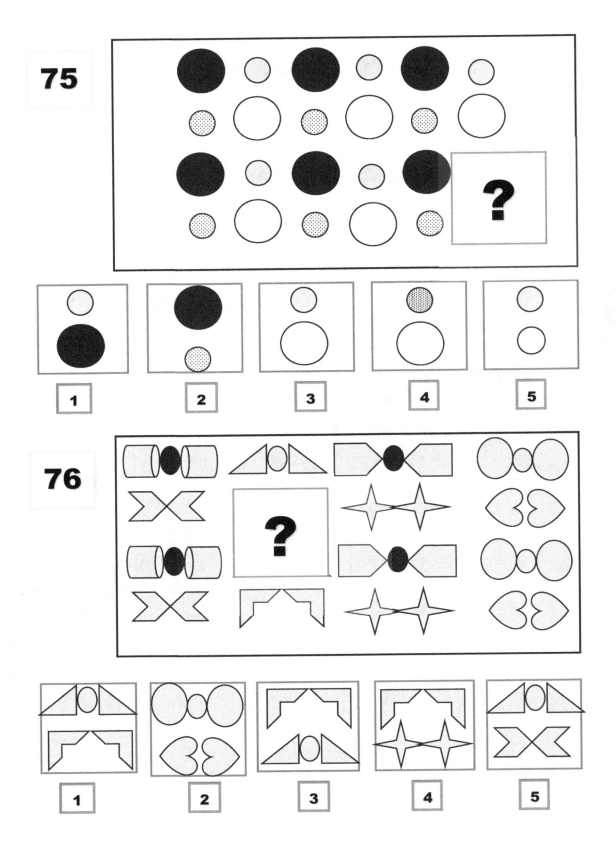

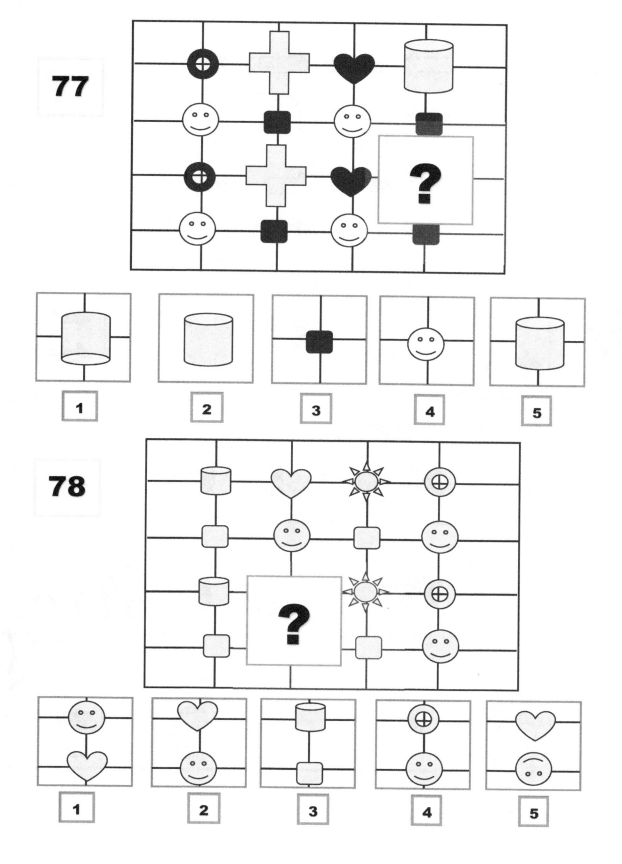

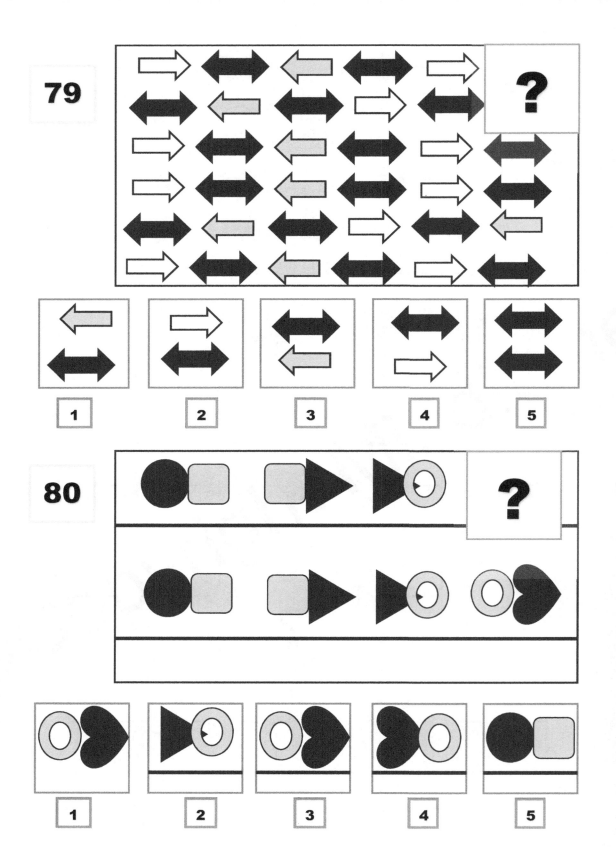

98

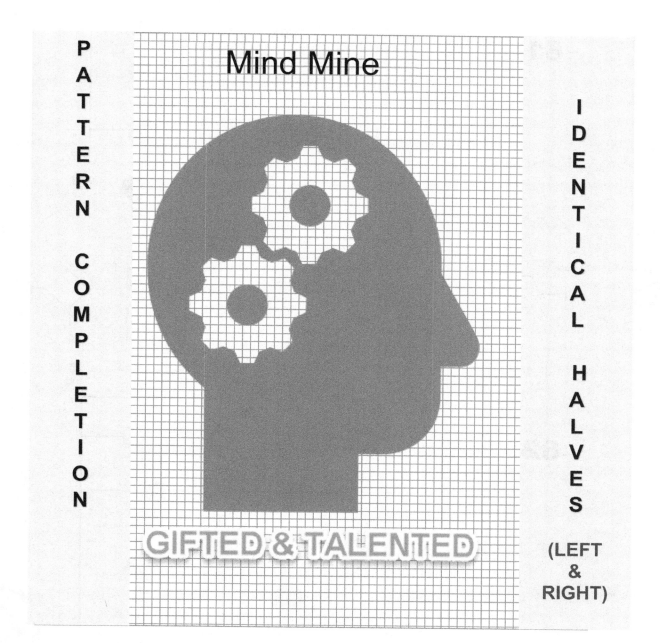

Mind Mine

GIFTED & TALENTED

IDENTICAL HALVES

(LEFT & RIGHT)

81

| 1 | 2 | 3 | 4 | 5 |

82

| 1 | 2 | 3 | 4 | 5 |

100

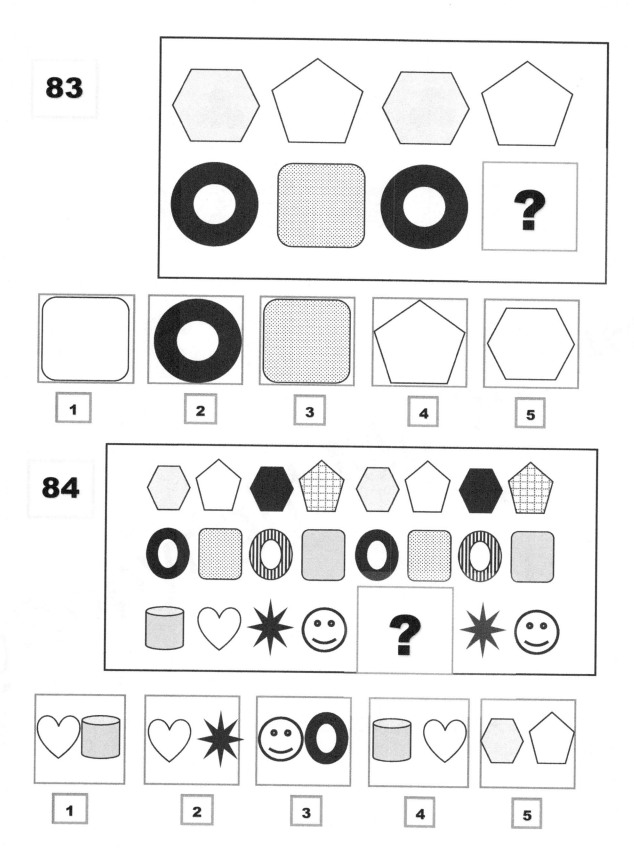

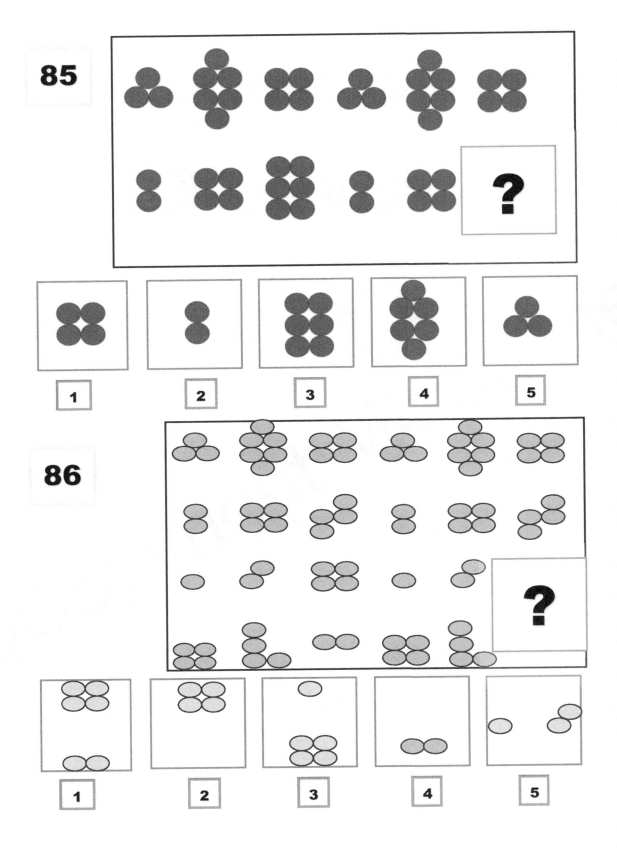

85

1 2 3 4 5

86

1 2 3 4 5

102

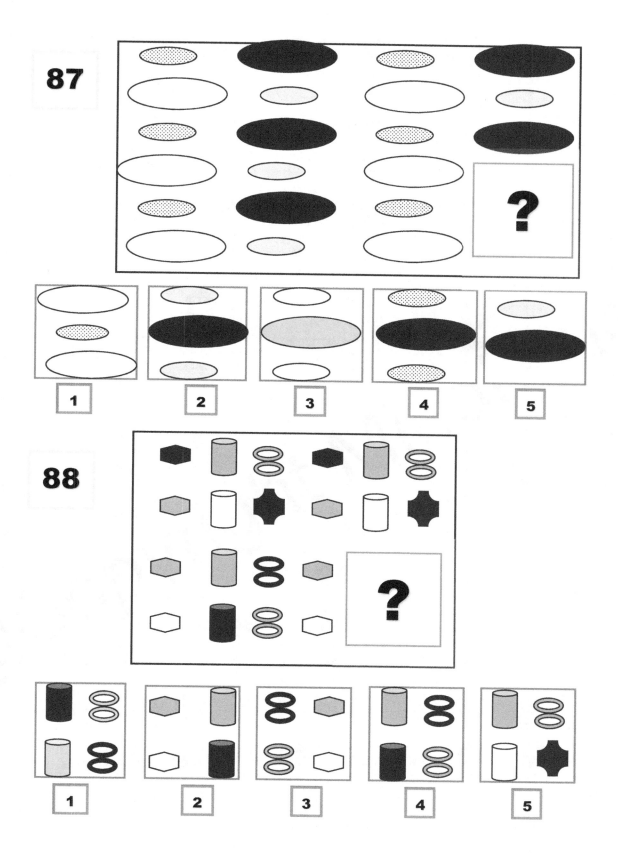

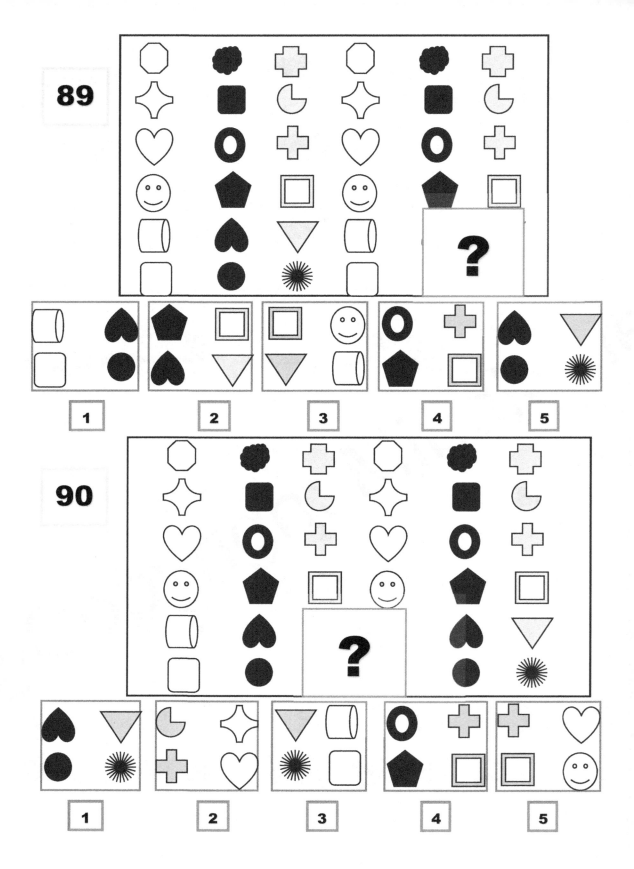

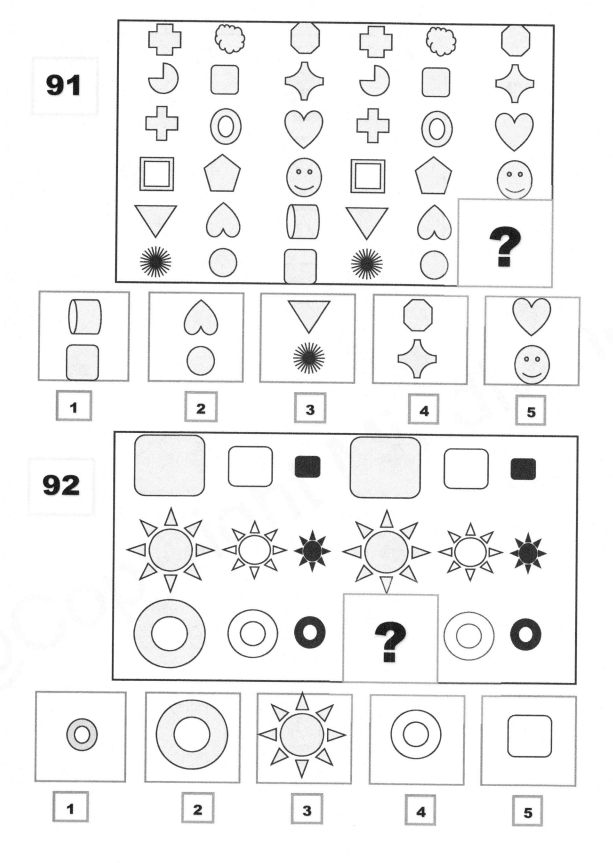

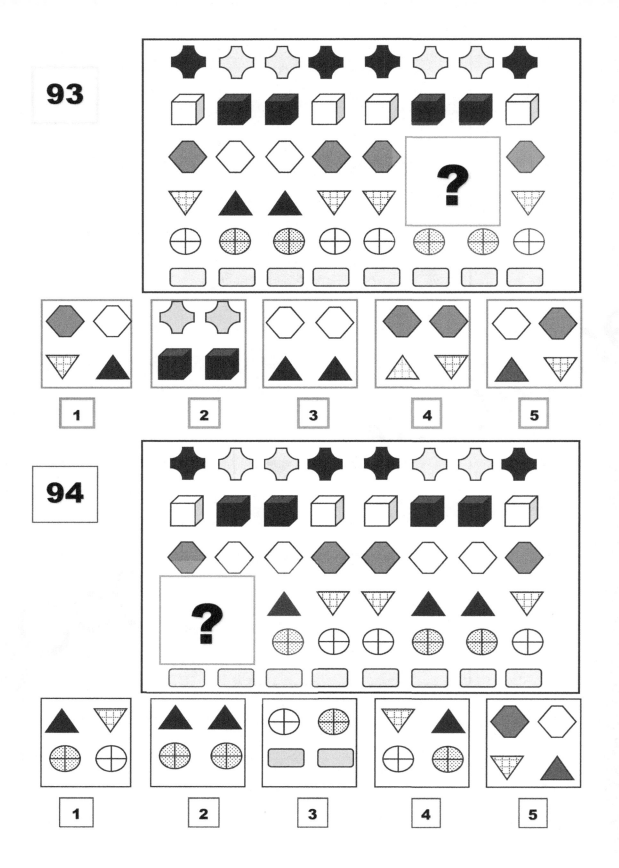

93

94

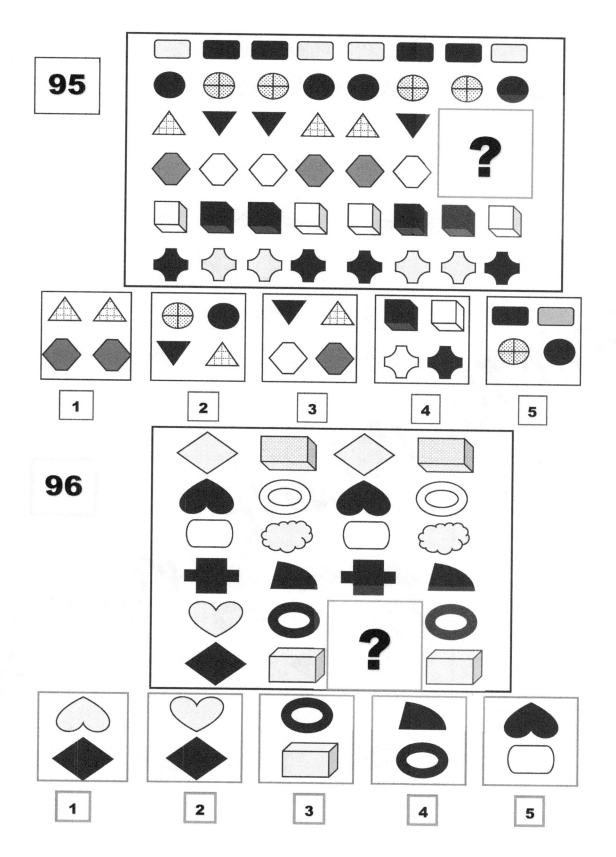

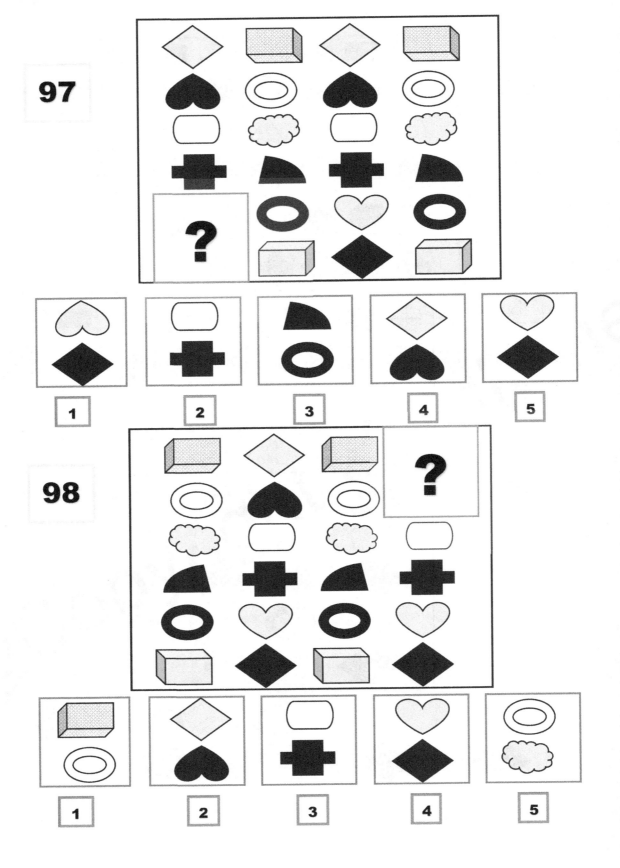

97

98

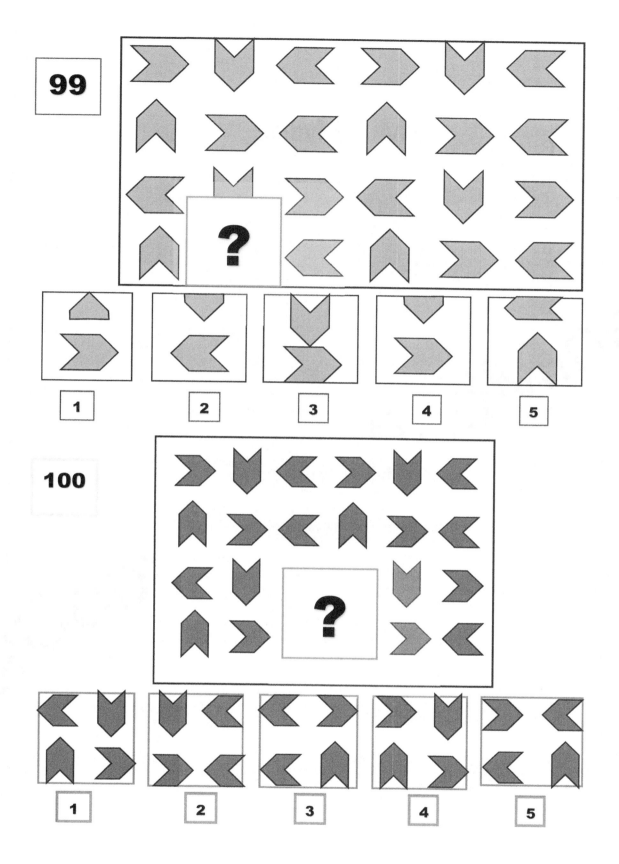

Mind Mine

RIGHT DIAGONAL

(Top-Left to Bottom-Right)

GIFTED & TALENTED

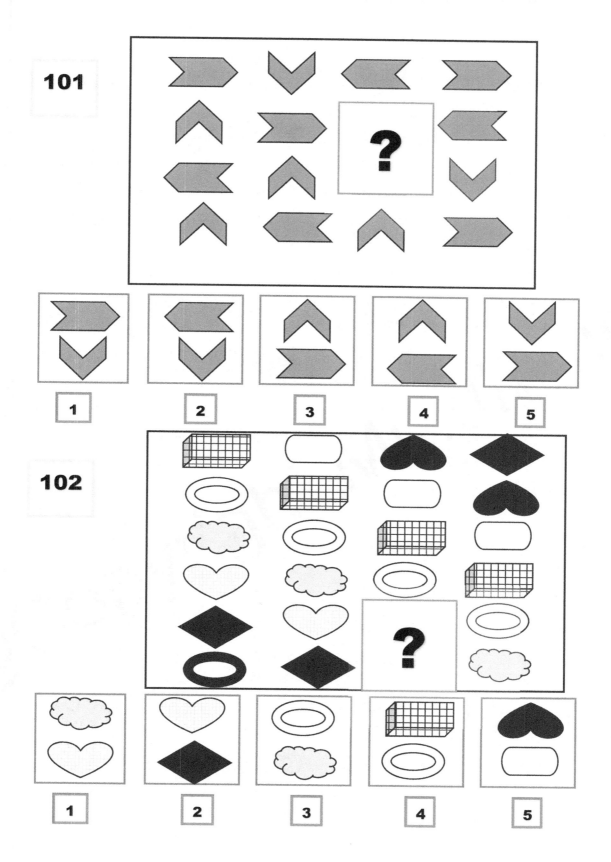

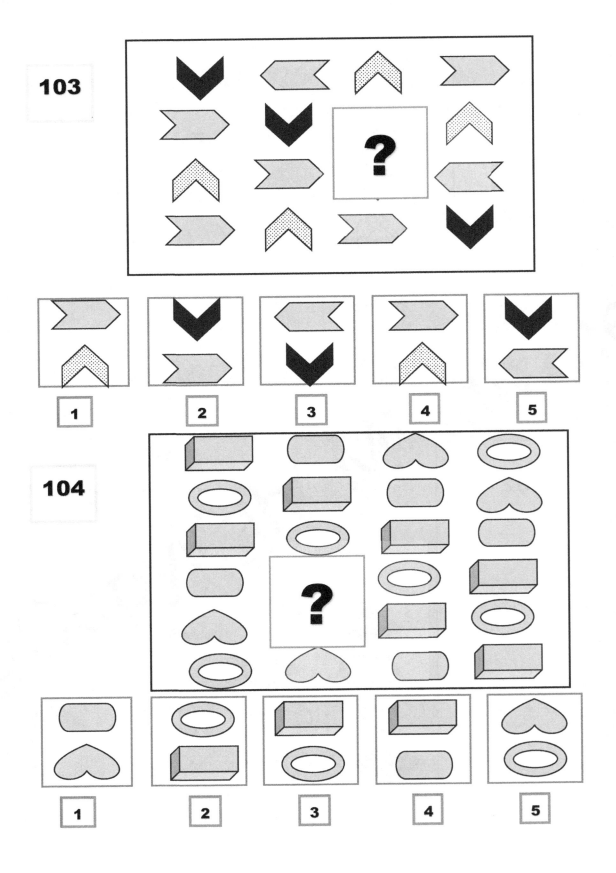

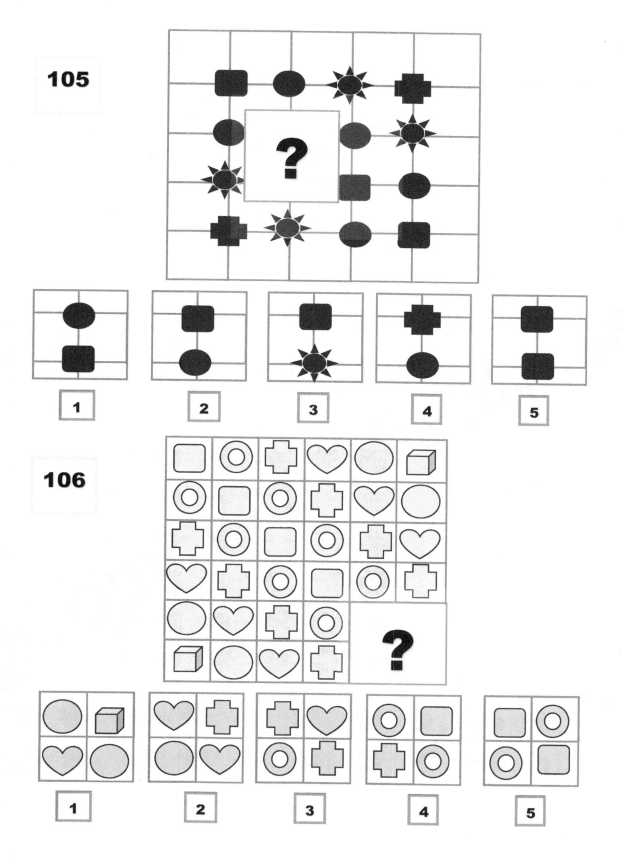

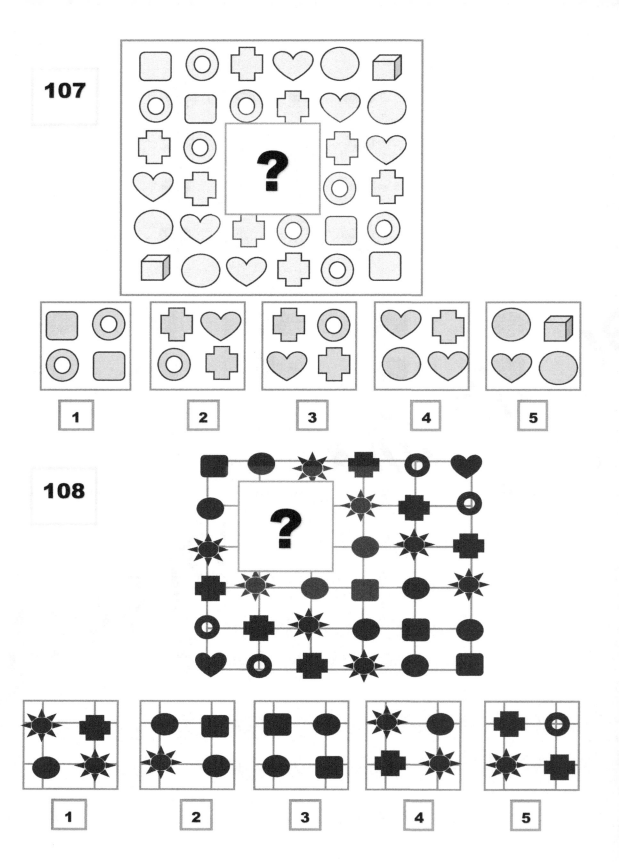

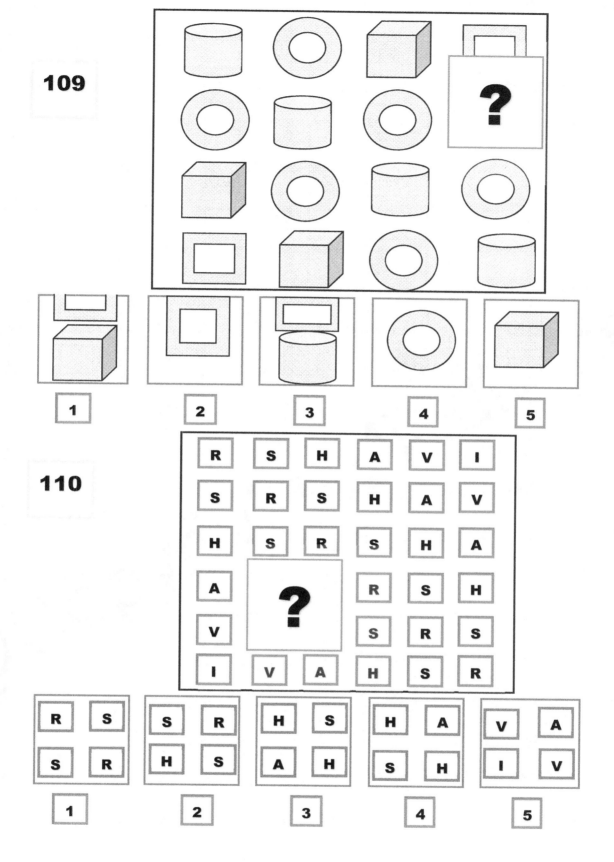

109

1   2   3   4   5

110

1   2   3   4   5

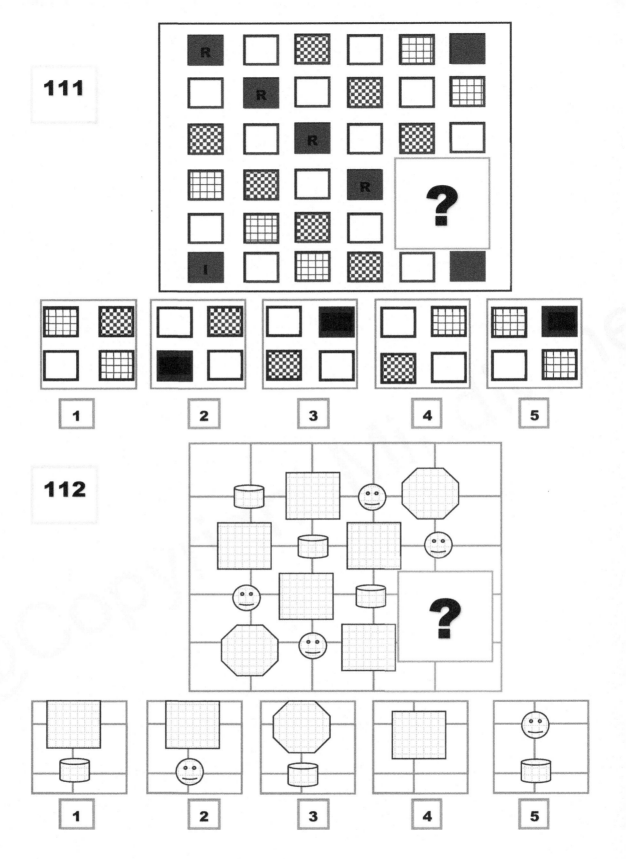

111

1   2   3   4   5

112

1   2   3   4   5

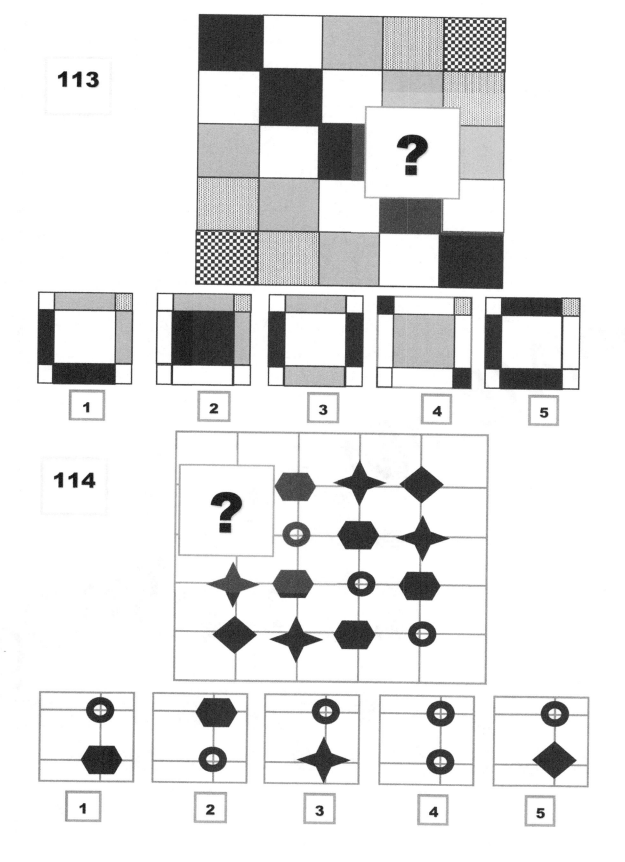

113

1 2 3 4 5

114

1 2 3 4 5

117

115

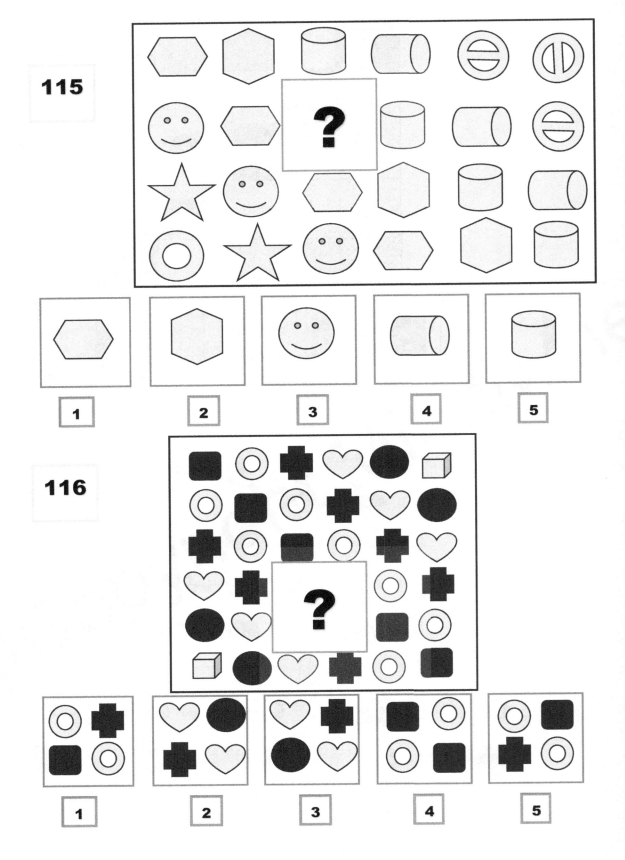

117

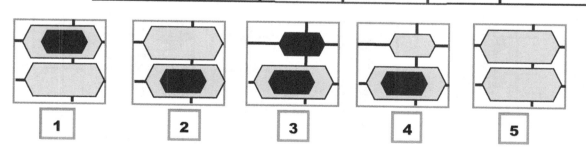

1 2 3 4 5

118

1 2 3 4 5

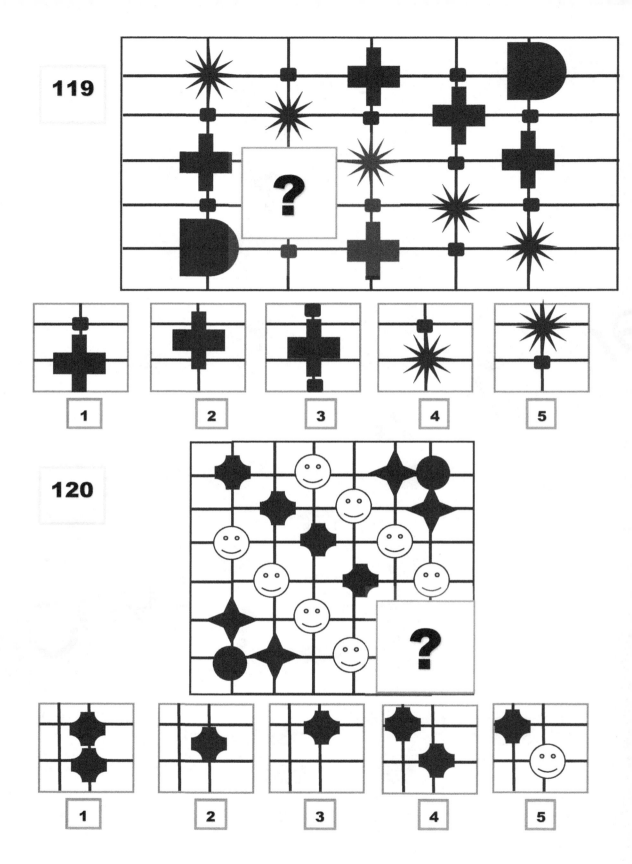

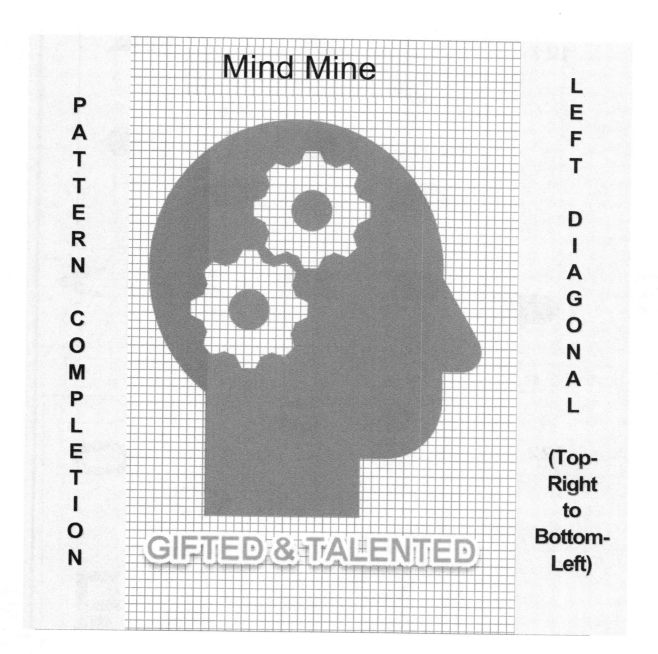

Mind Mine

LEFT DIAGONAL

(Top-Right to Bottom-Left)

GIFTED & TALENTED

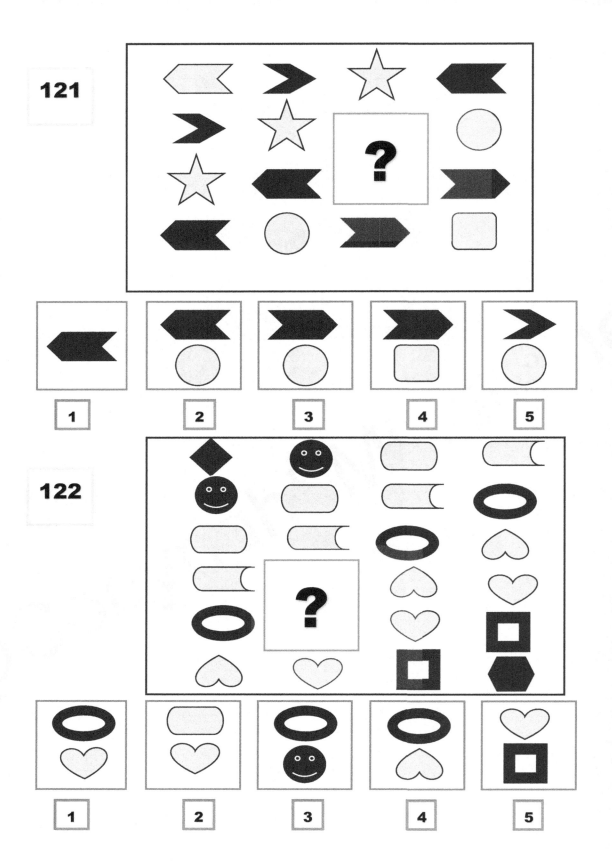

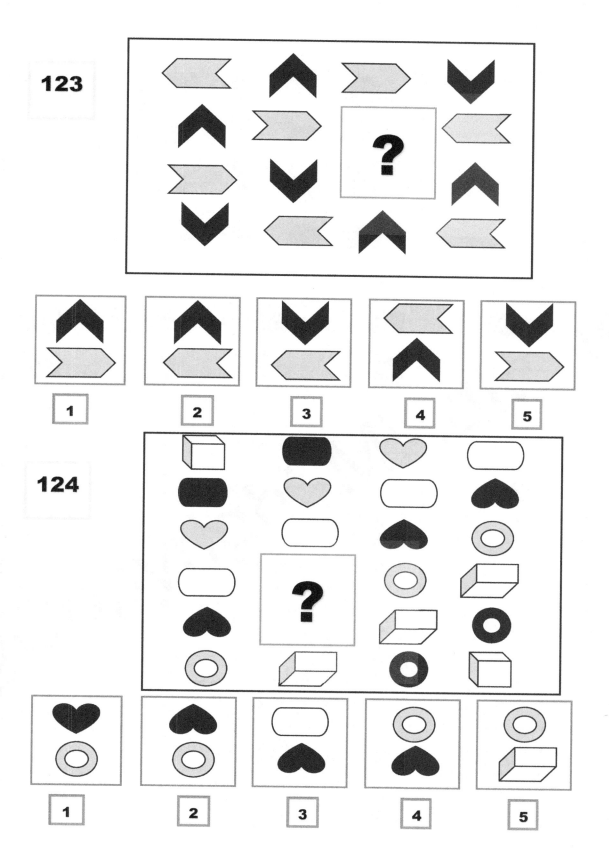

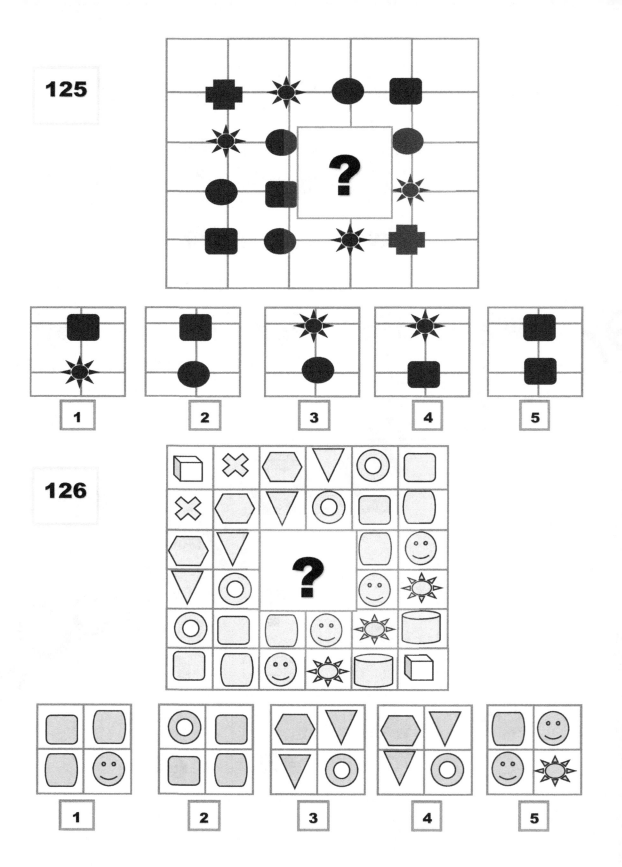

125

126

124

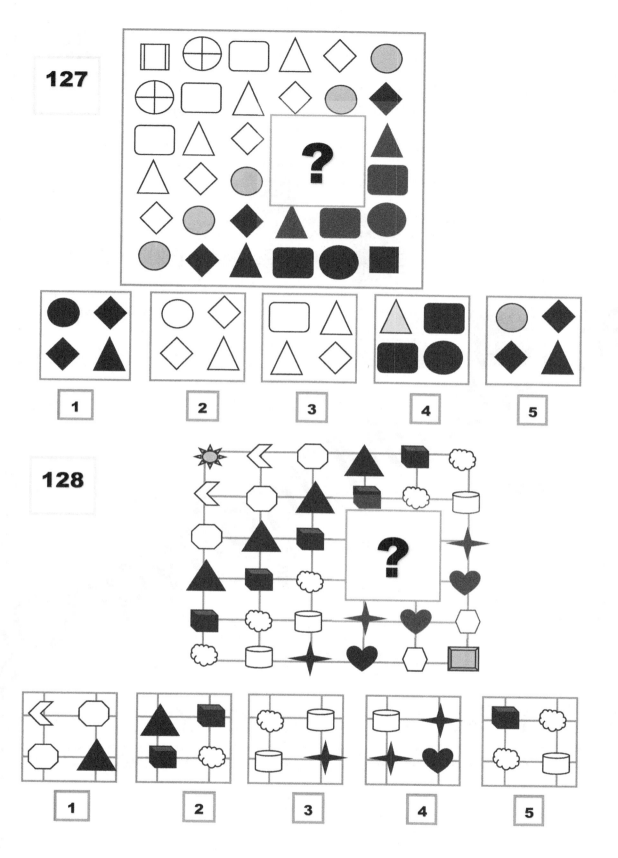

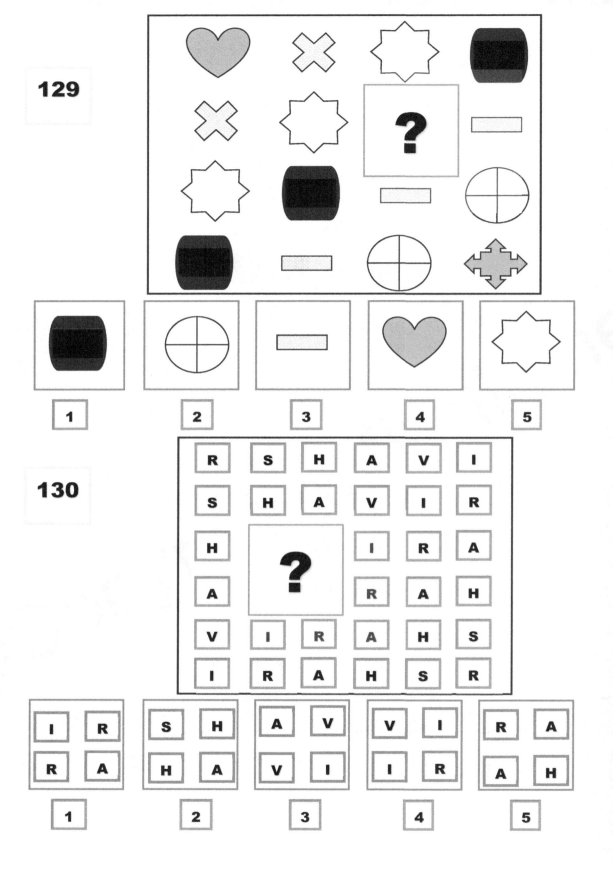

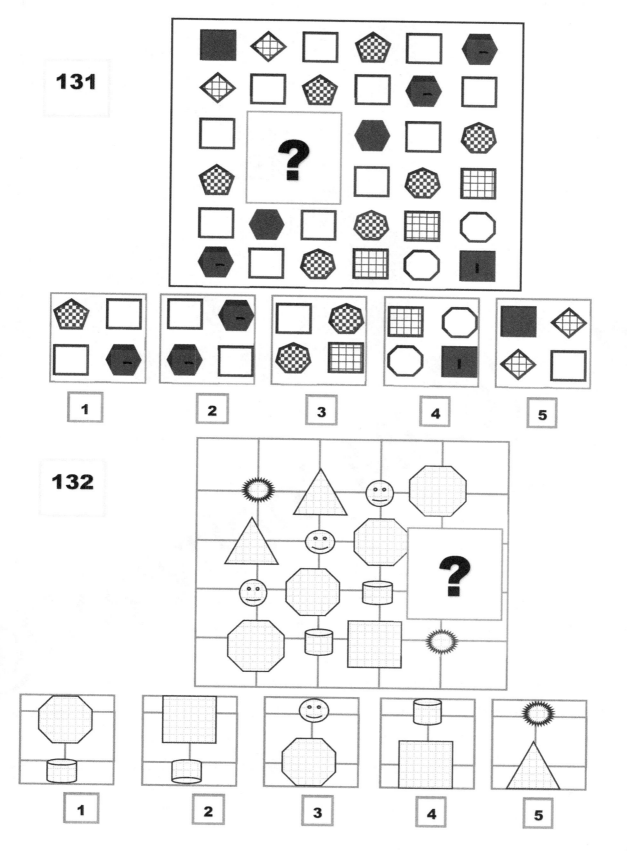

133

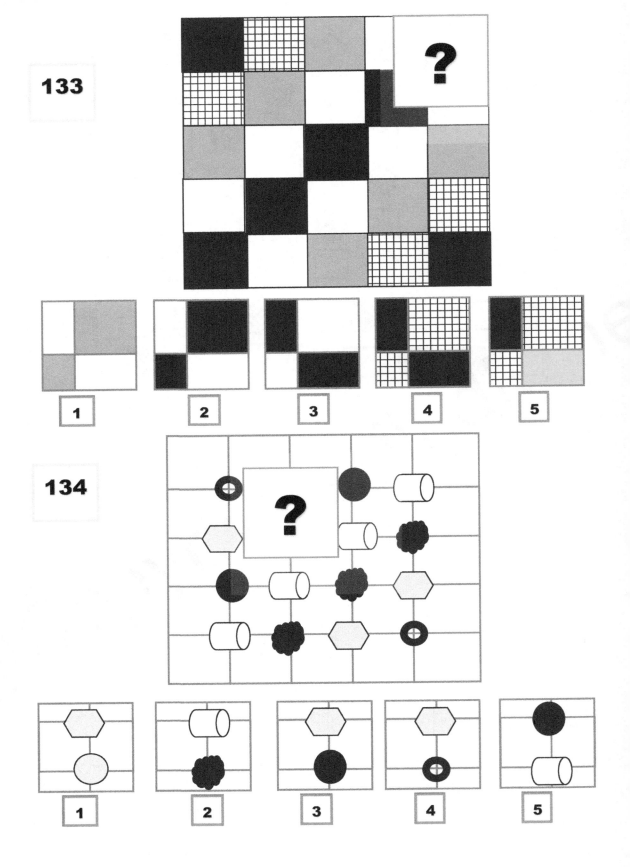

1   **2**   **3**   **4**   **5**

134

1   **2**   **3**   **4**   **5**

128

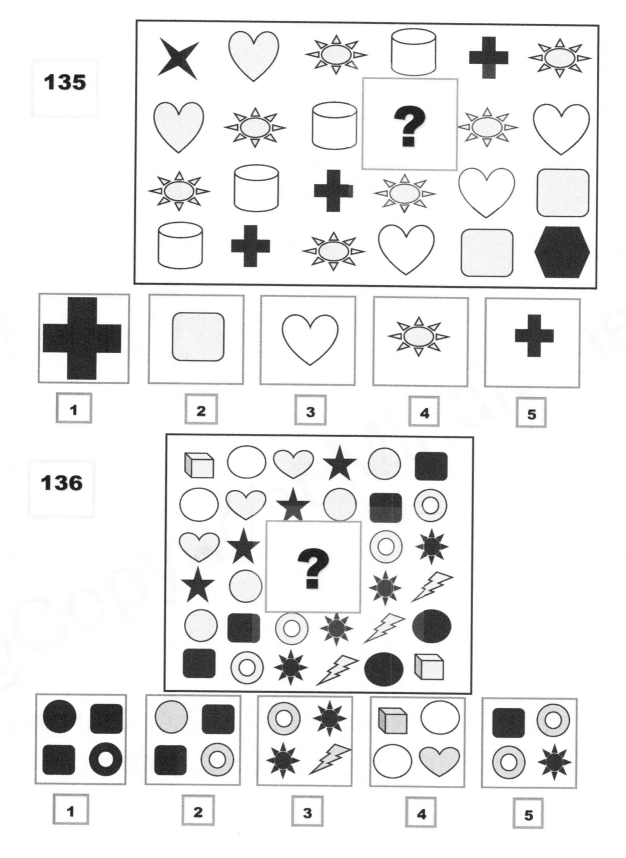

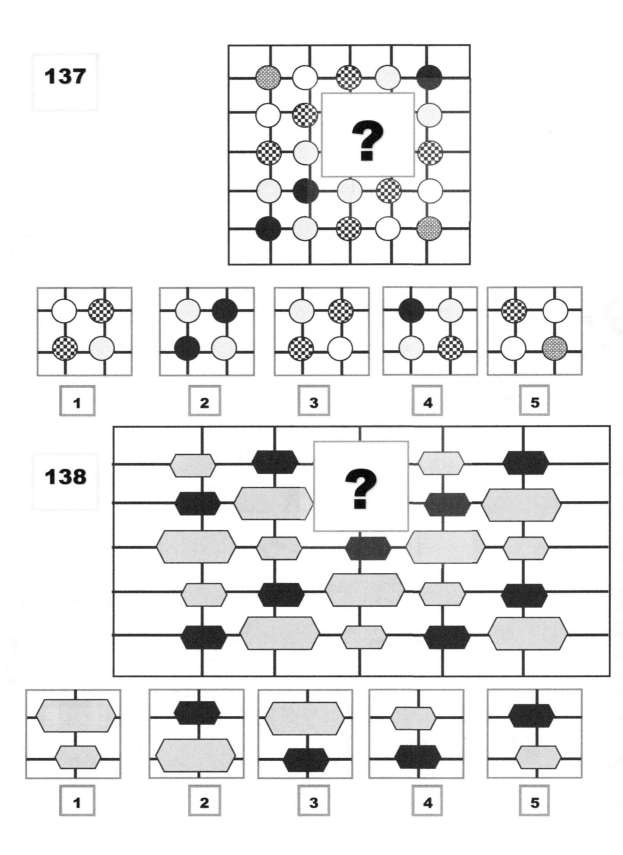

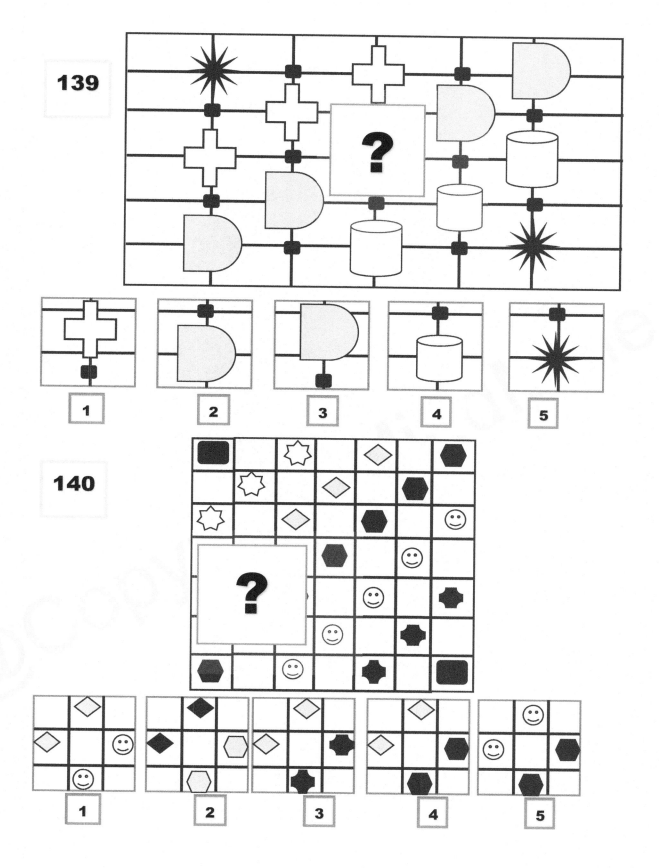

139

140

Mind Mine

PATTERN COMPLETION

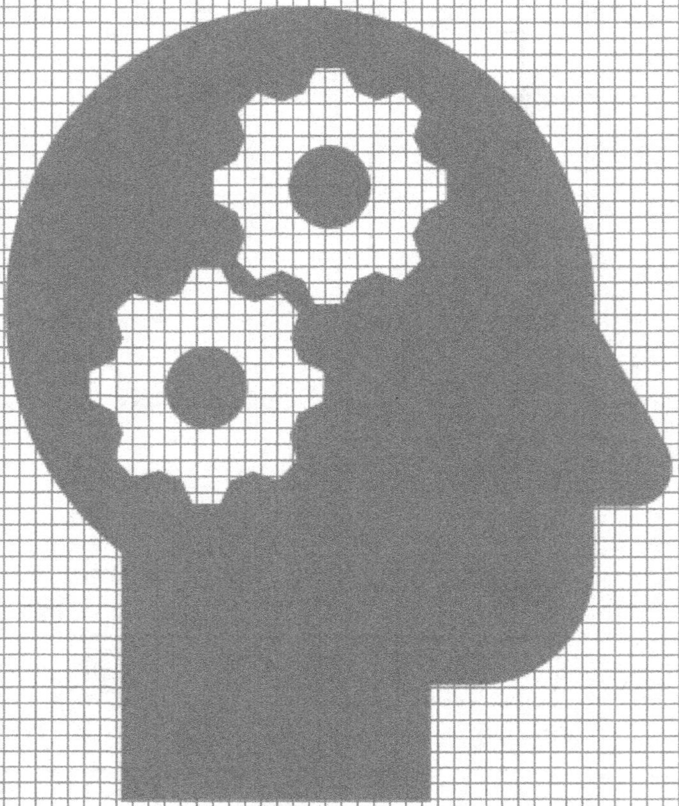

GIFTED & TALENTED

REPEATING COLUMNS

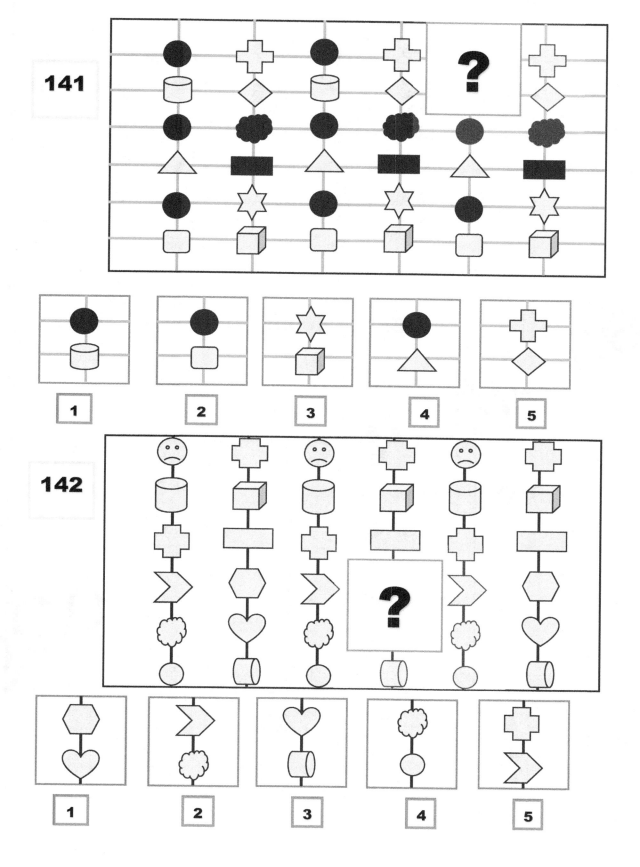

133

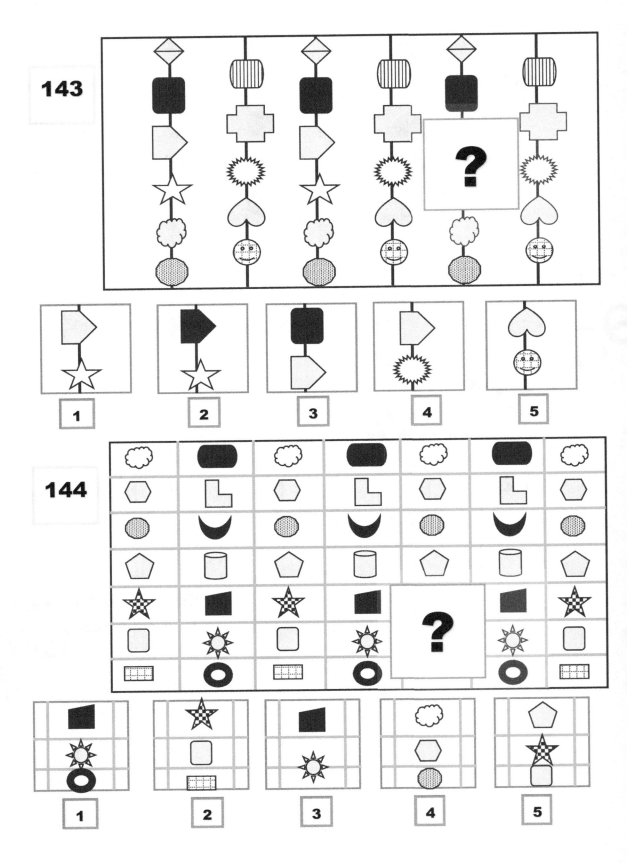

134

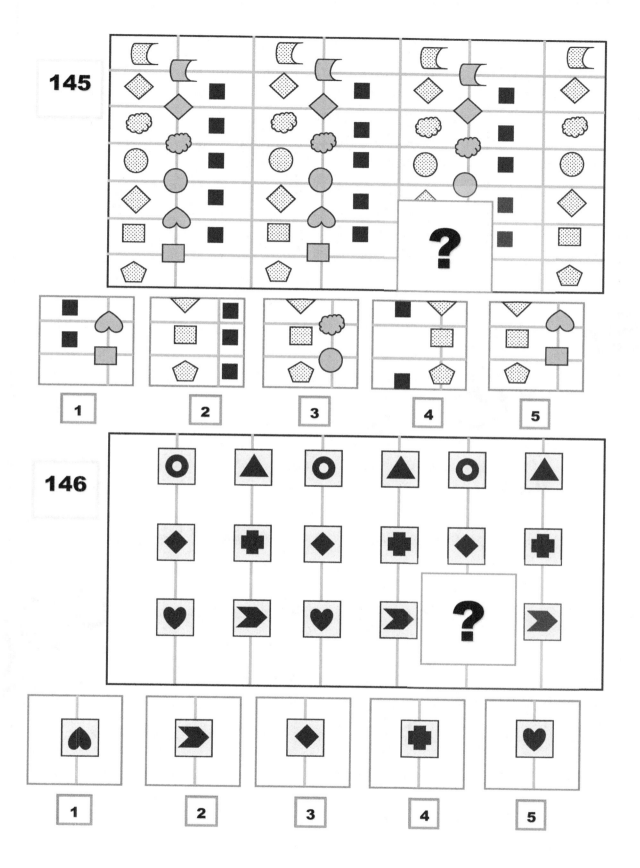

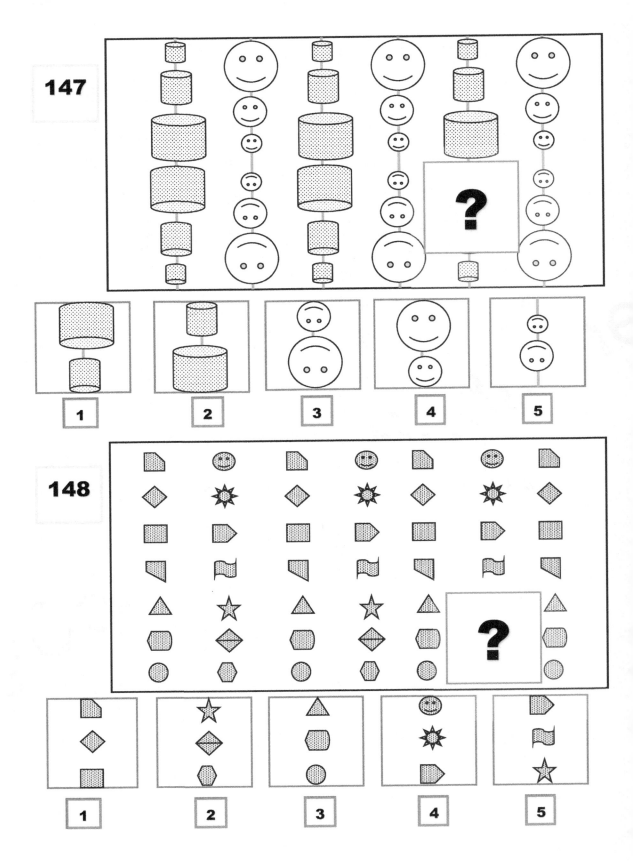

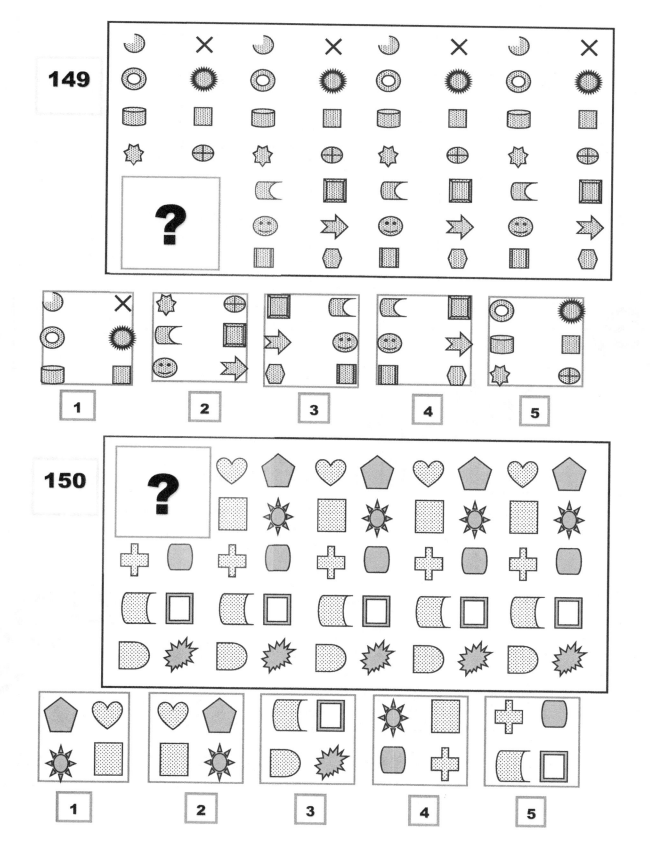

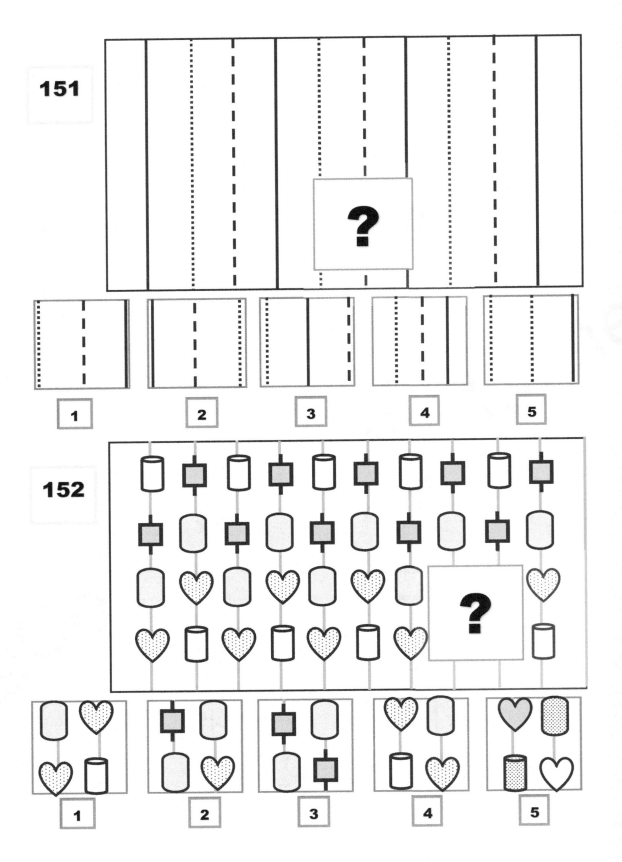

151

1   2   3   4   5

152

1   2   3   4   5

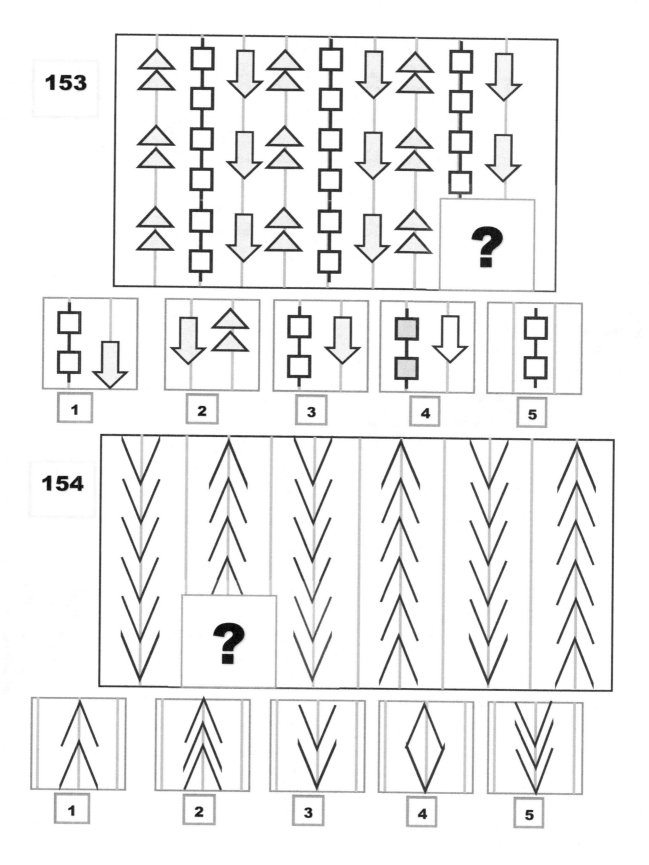

153

154

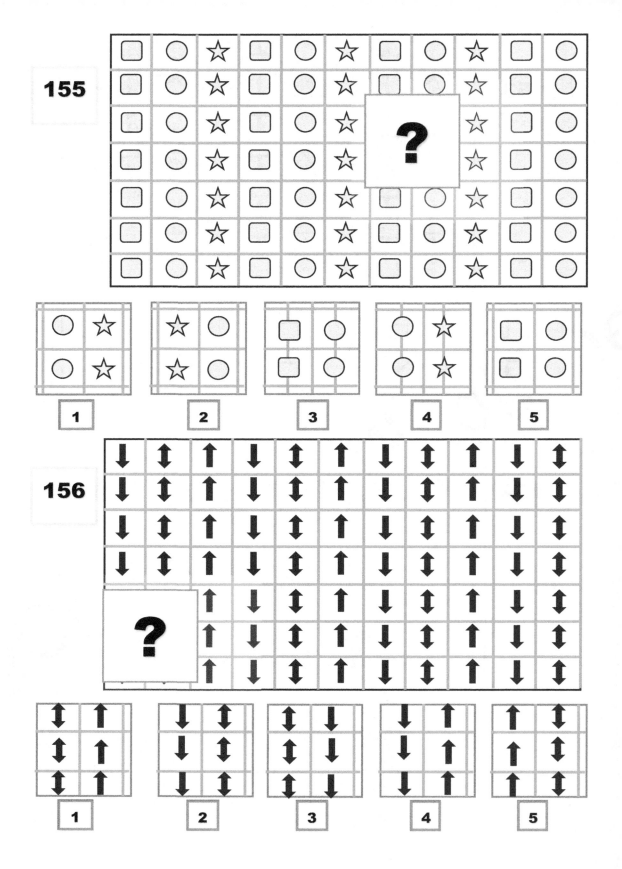

155

156

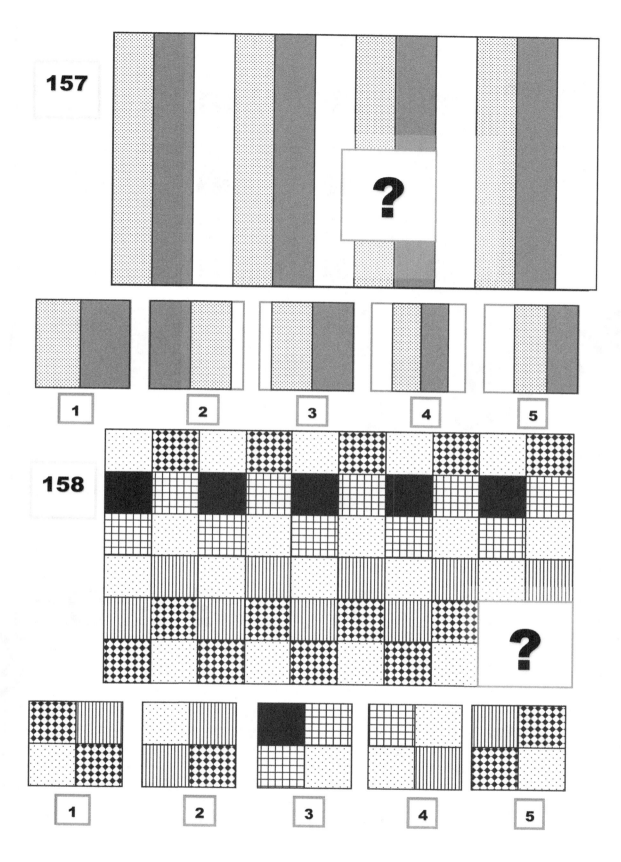

157

158

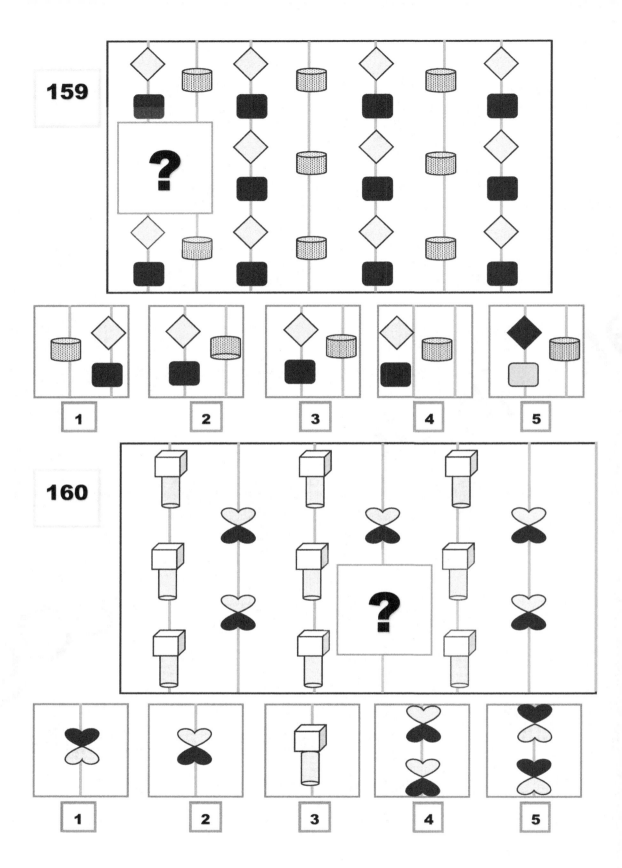

Mind Mine

PATTERN COMPLETION

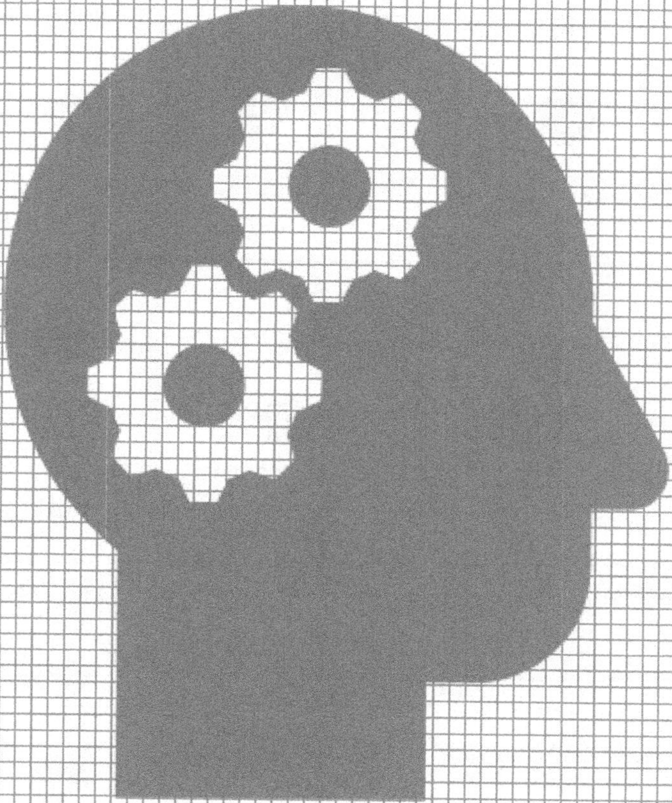

REPEATING ROWS

GIFTED & TALENTED

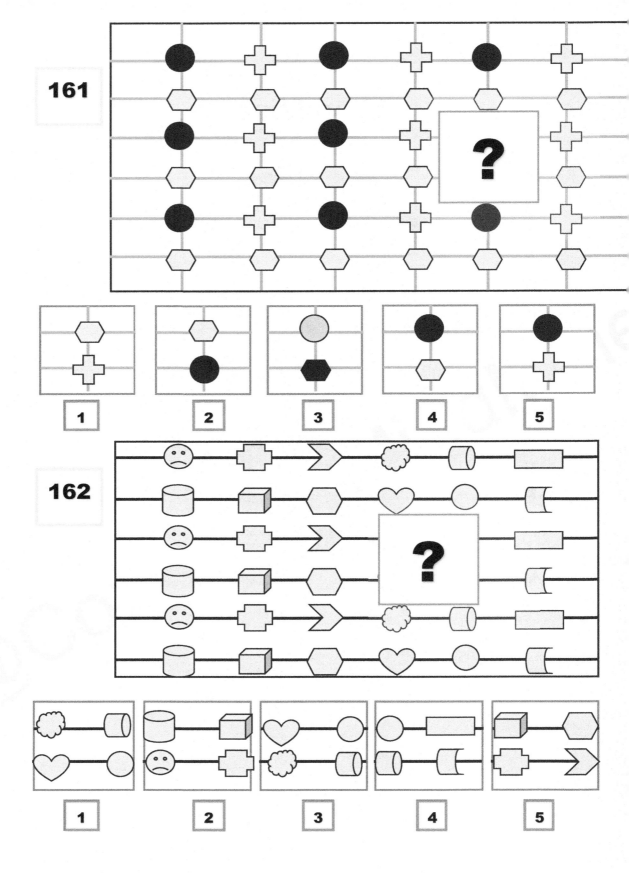

161

1   2   3   4   5

162

1   2   3   4   5

144

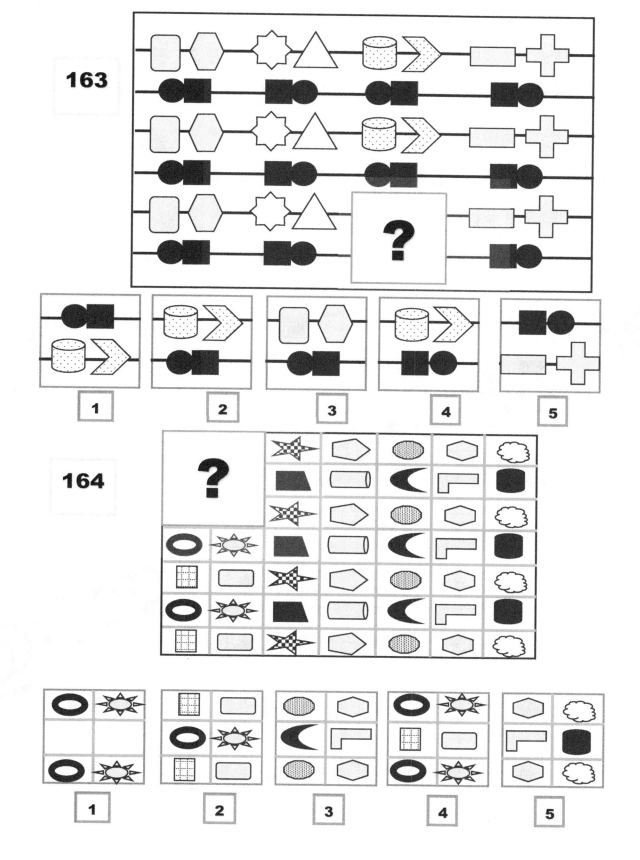

163

164

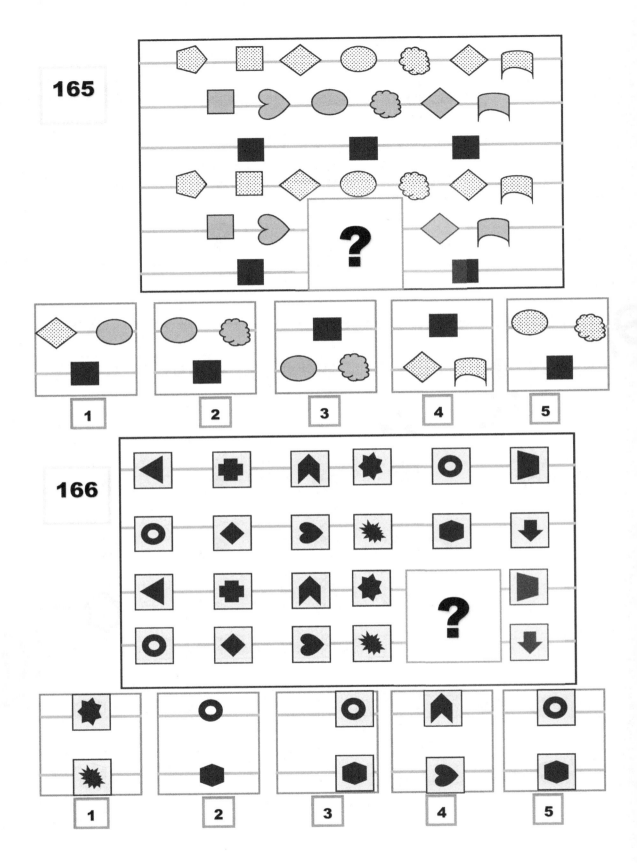

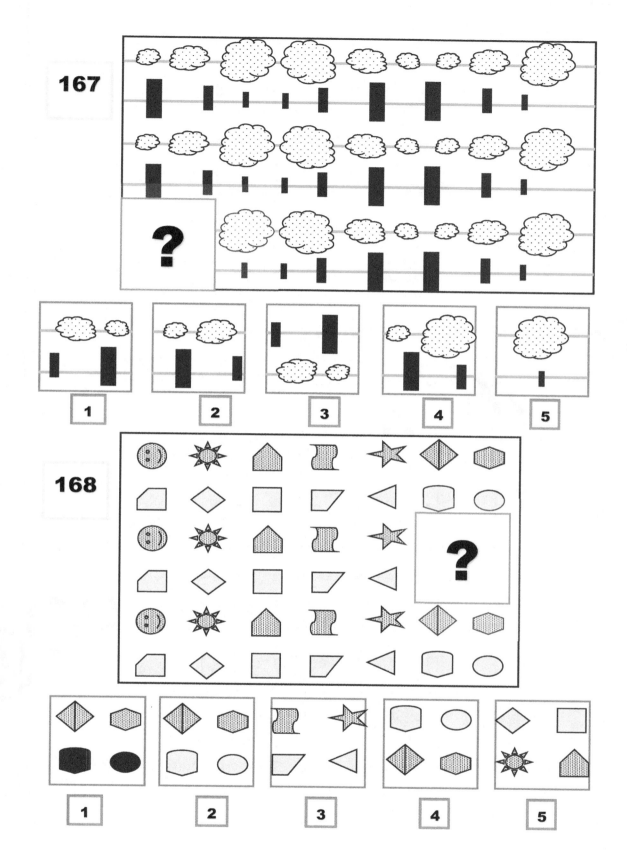

167

168

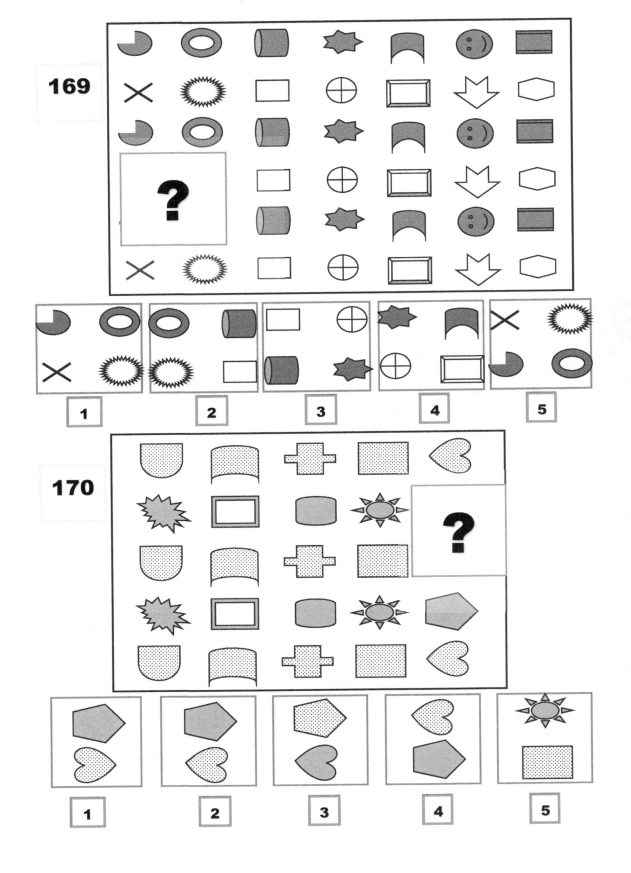

169

1   2   3   4   5

170

1   2   3   4   5

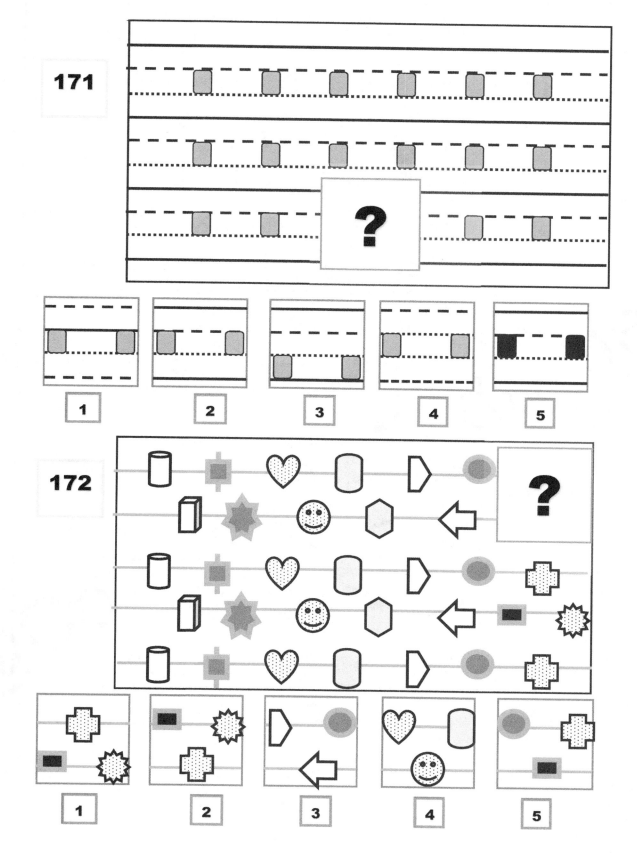

171

1   2   3   4   5

172

1   2   3   4   5

149

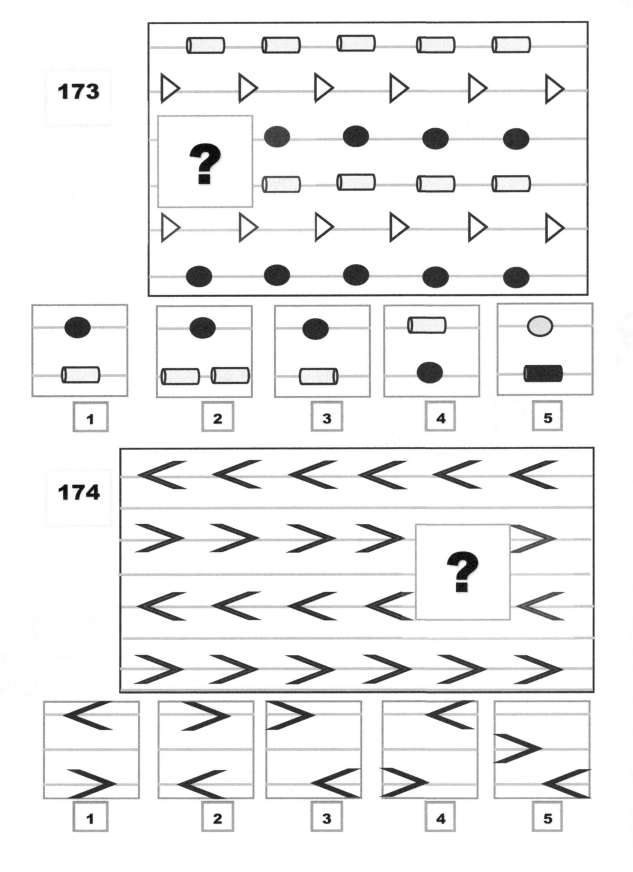

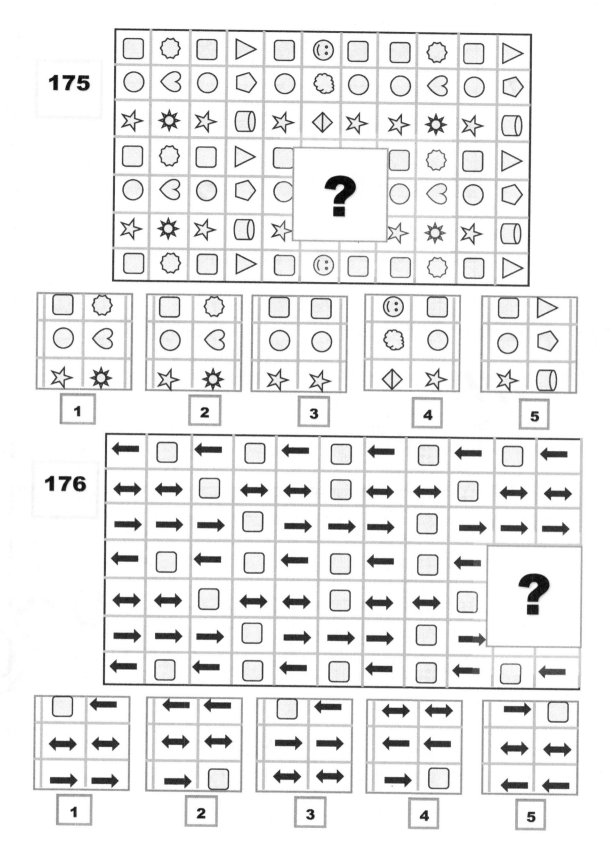

151

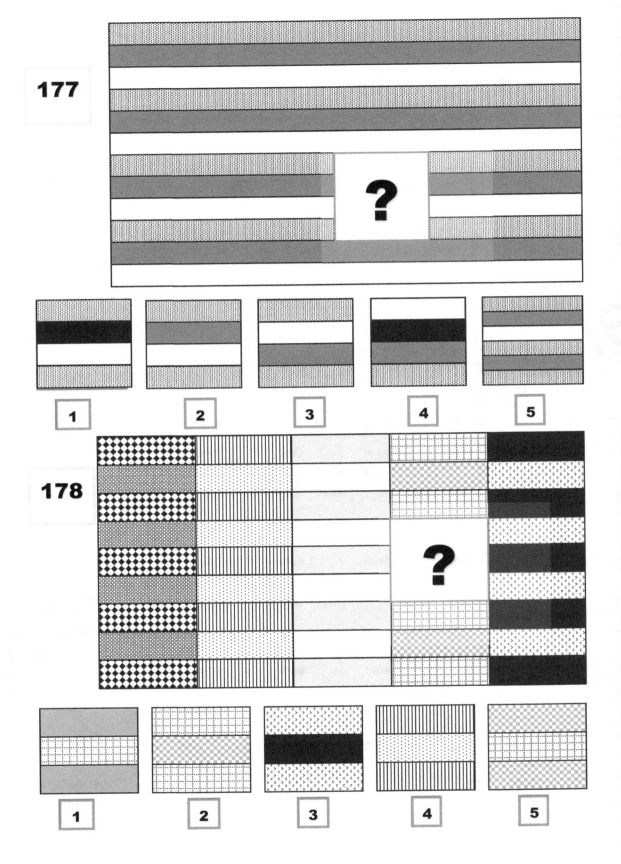

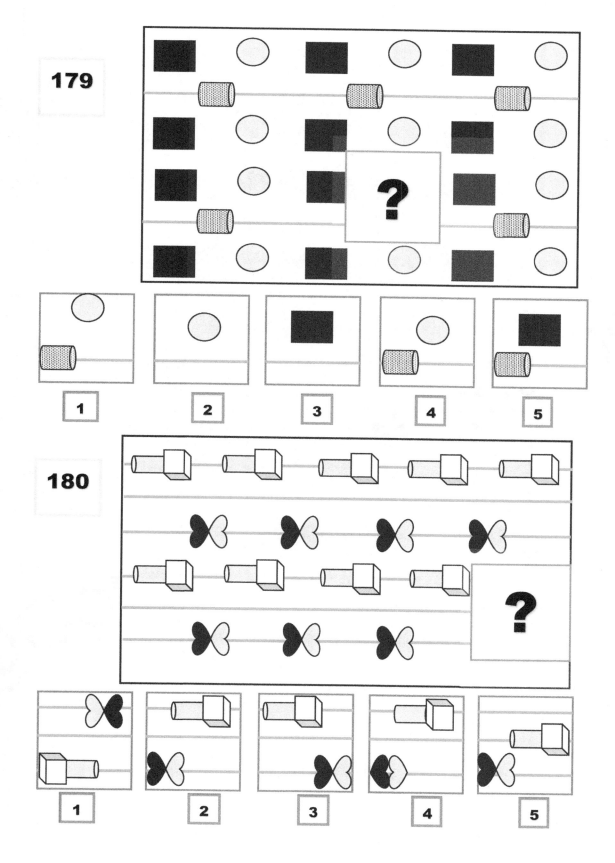

Mind Mine

PATTERN COMPLETION

PRACTICE TEST #1

GIFTED & TALENTED

1

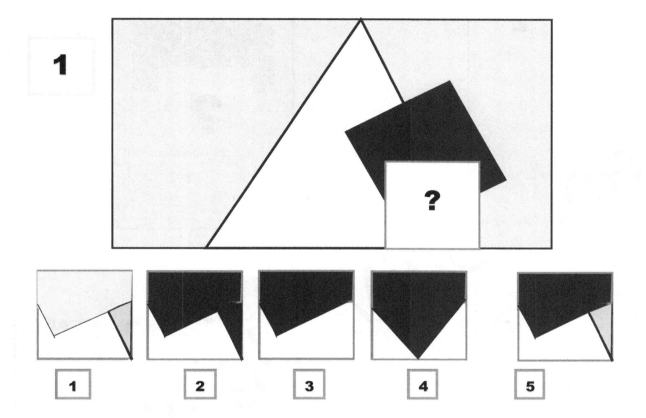

2

3

157

4

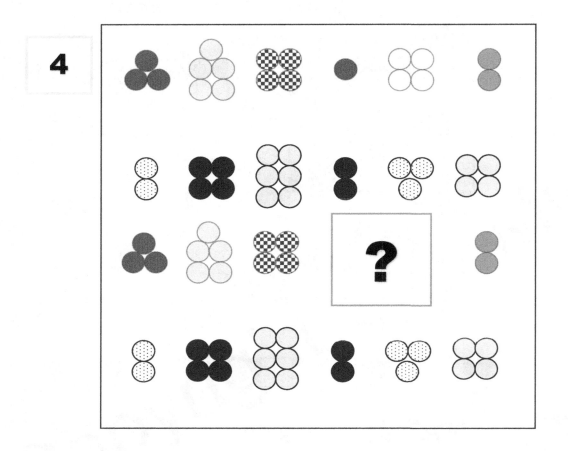

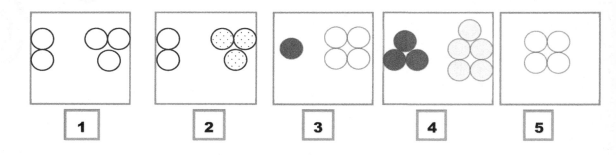

5

6

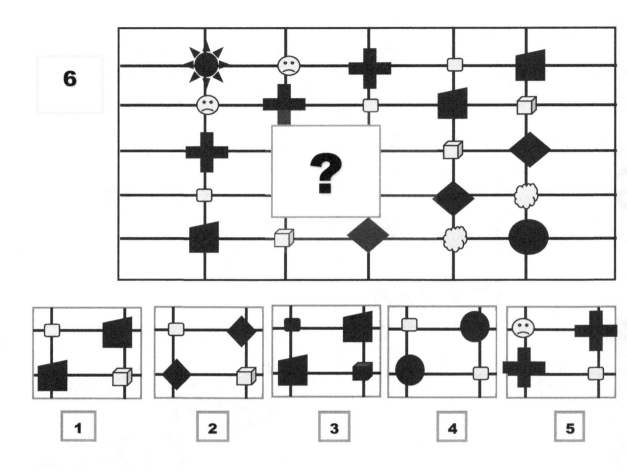

7

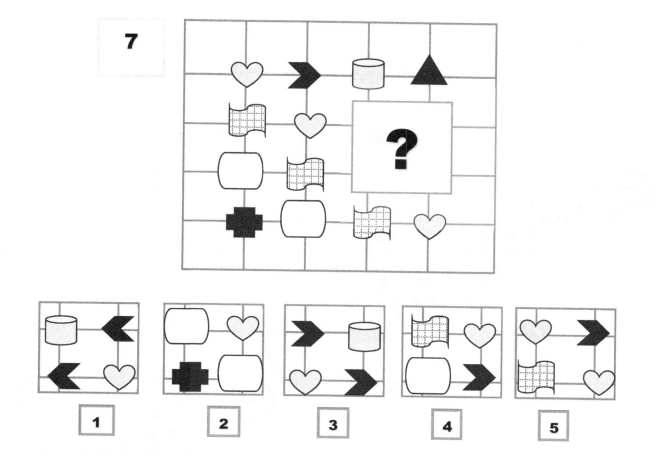

8

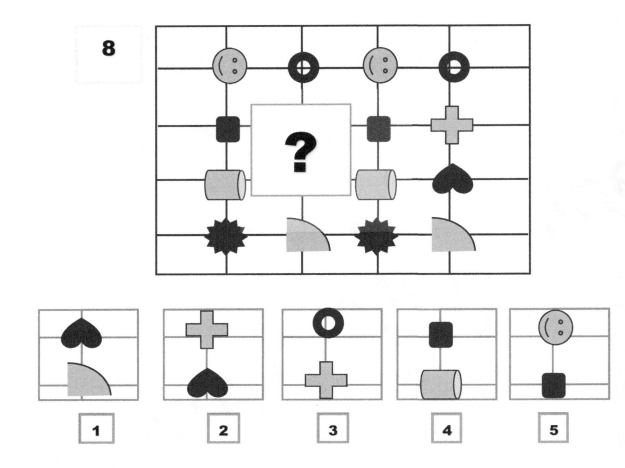

162

9

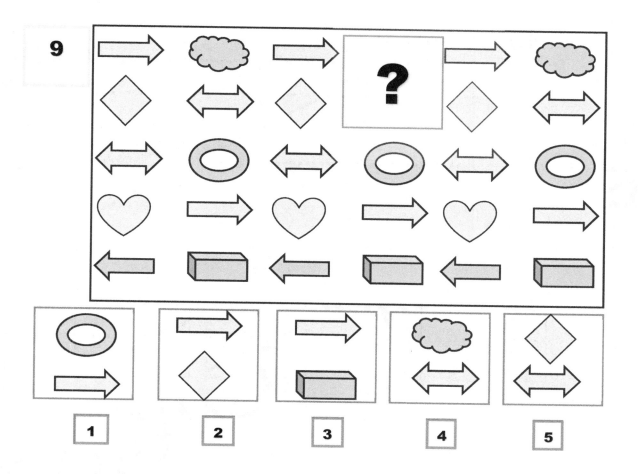

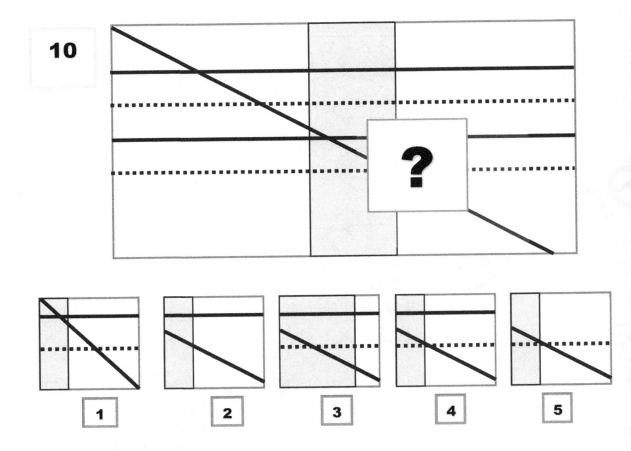

Mind Mine

GIFTED & TALENTED

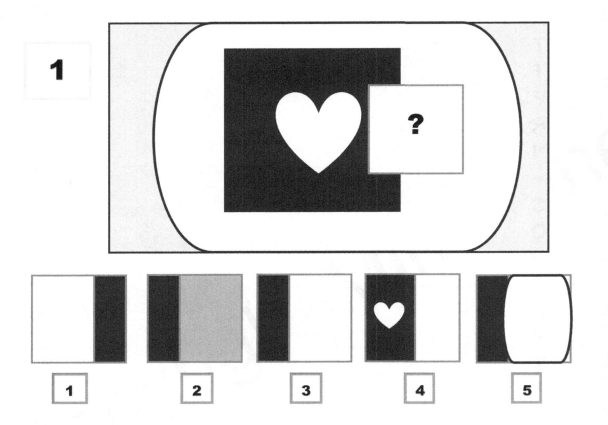

166

2

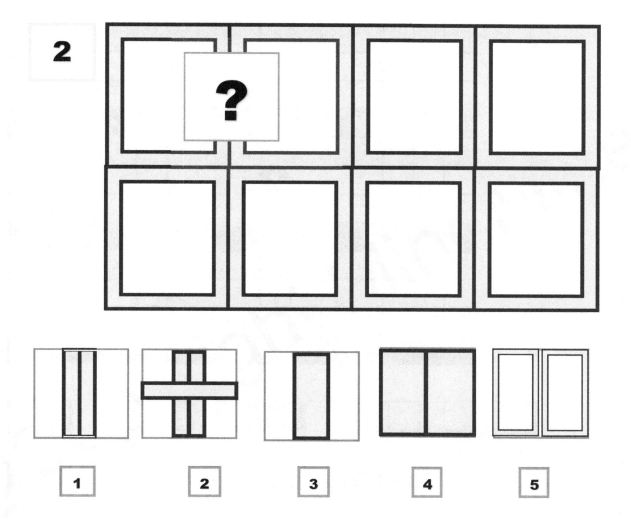

| 1 | 2 | 3 | 4 | 5 |

167

3

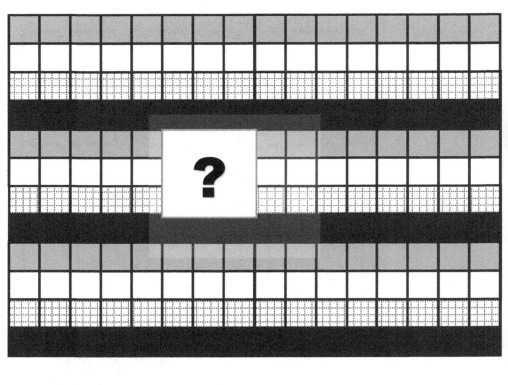

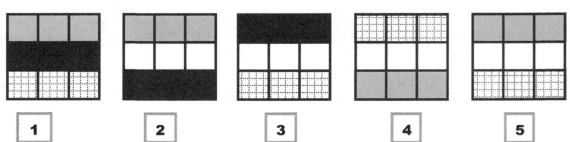

| 1 | 2 | 3 | 4 | 5 |

4

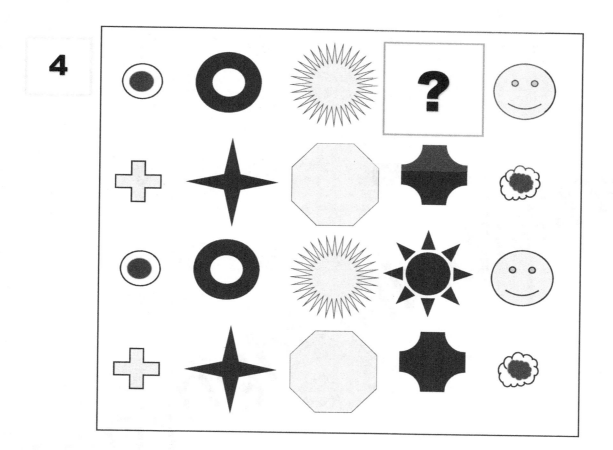

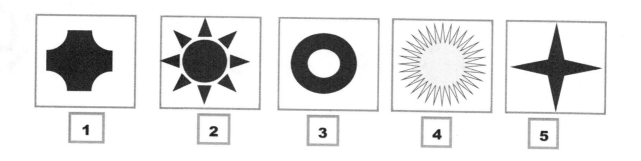

169

5

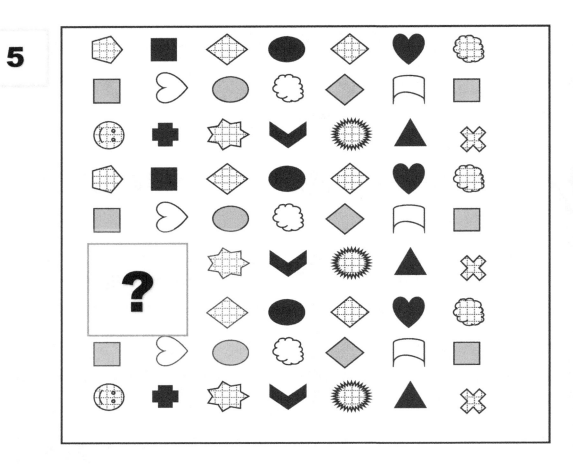

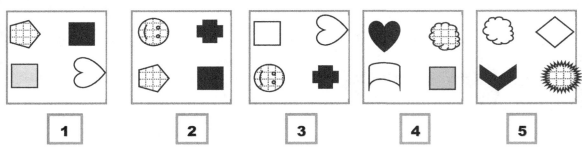

6

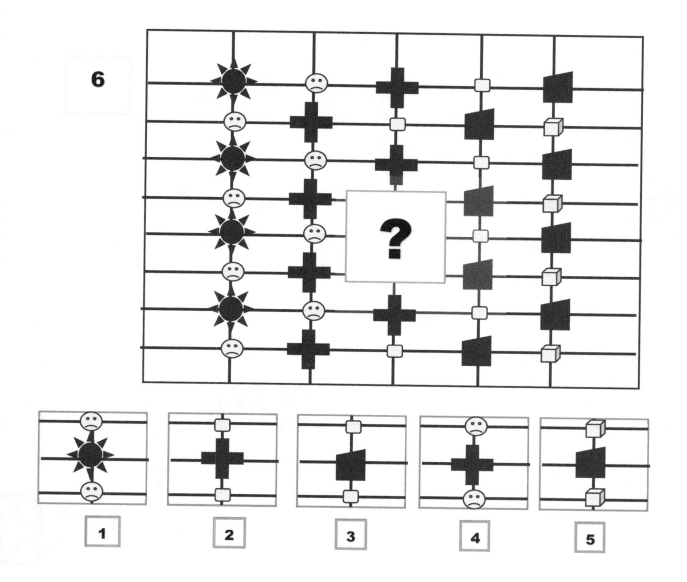

171

7

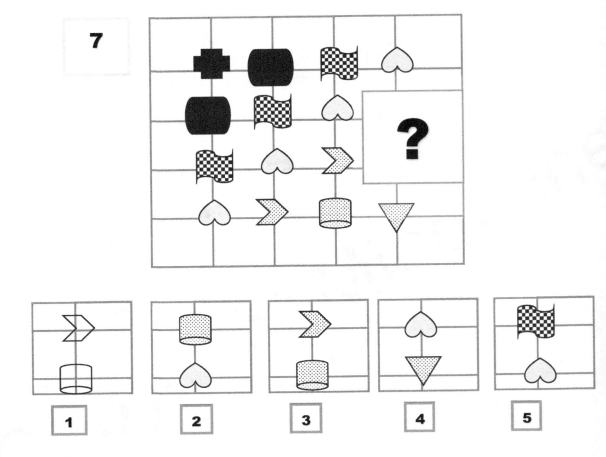

172

8

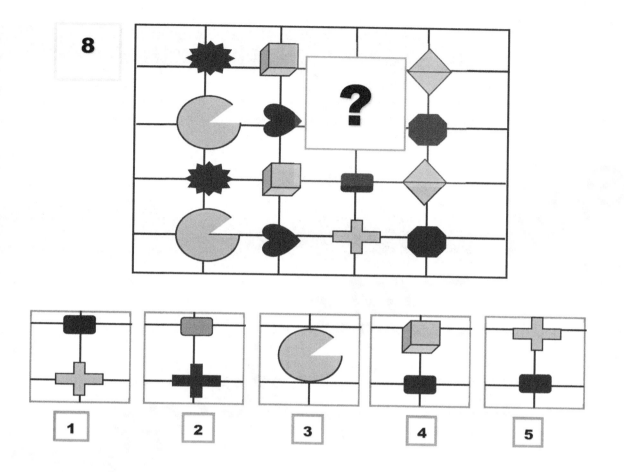

173

9

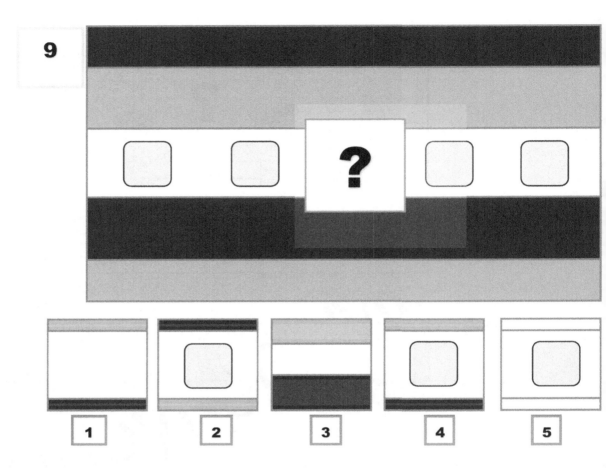

174

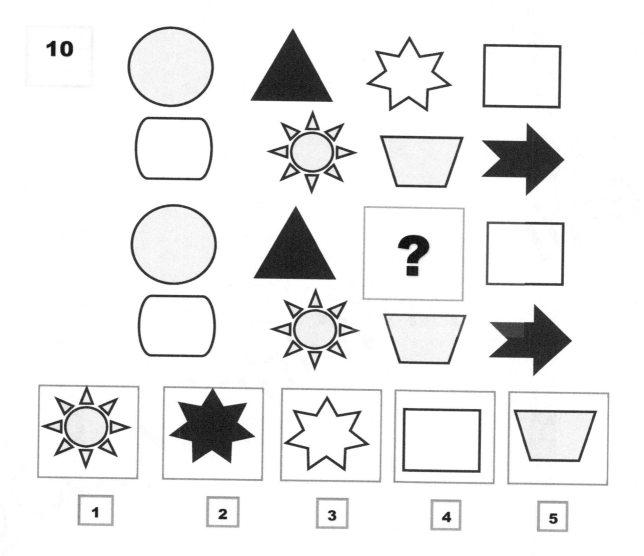

ANSWERS

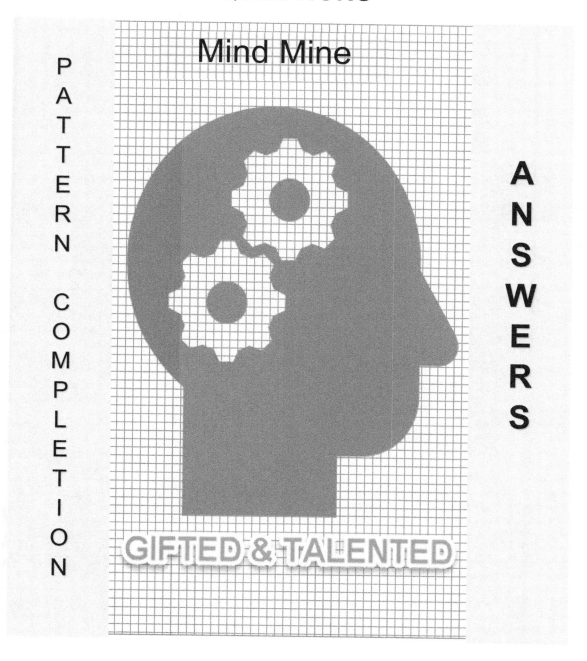

Mind Mine

PATTERN COMPLETION

ANSWERS

GIFTED & TALENTED

QUESTION	ANSWER

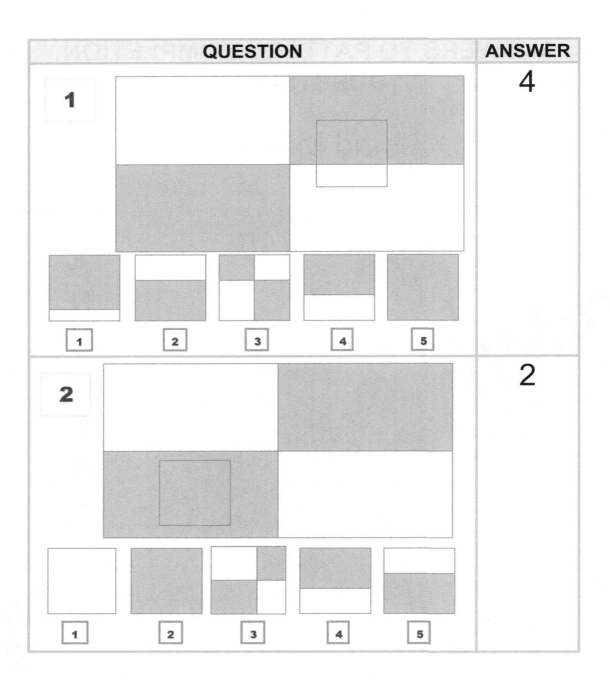

1	4
2	2

QUESTION	ANSWER

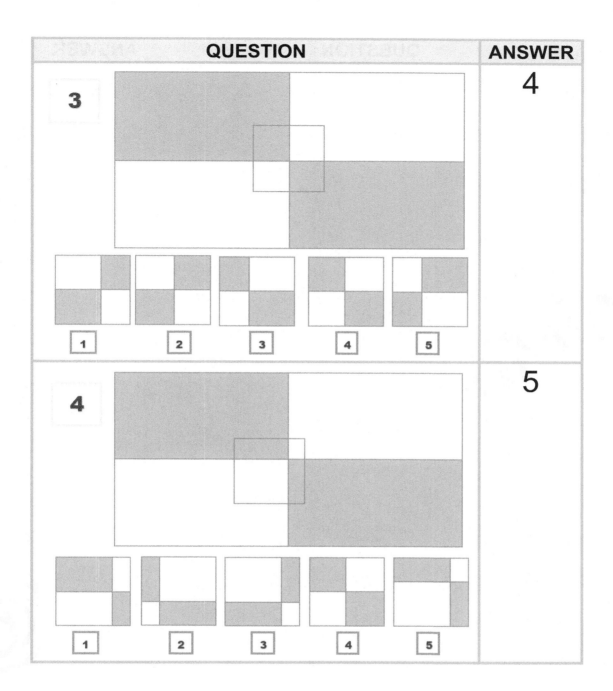

3

1 2 3 4 5

Answer: 4

4

1 2 3 4 5

Answer: 5

QUESTION	ANSWER
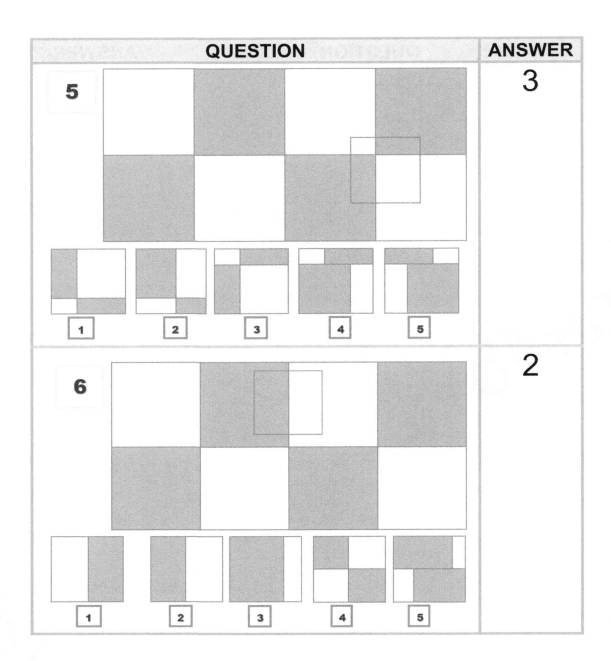	3
	2

QUESTION	ANSWER
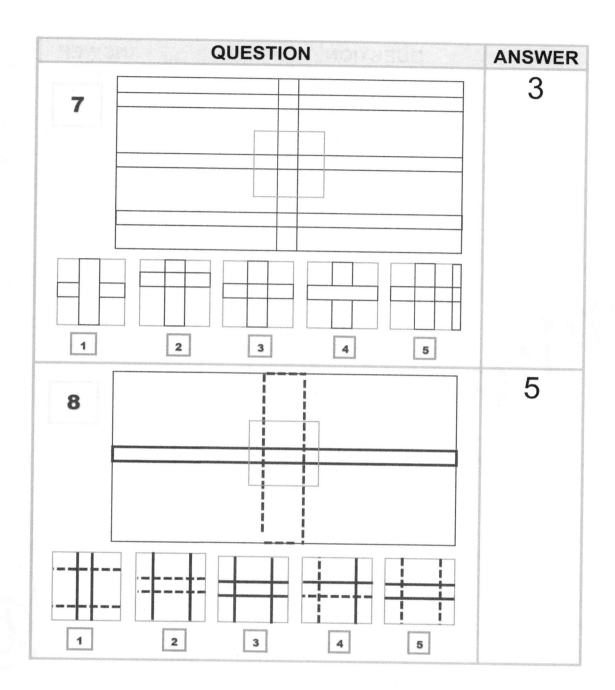	3
	5

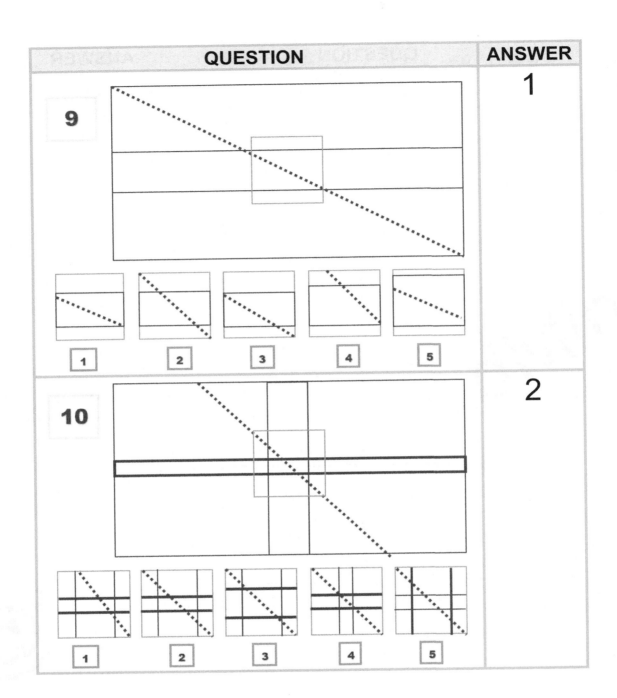

ANSWER

1

2

QUESTION	ANSWER

11

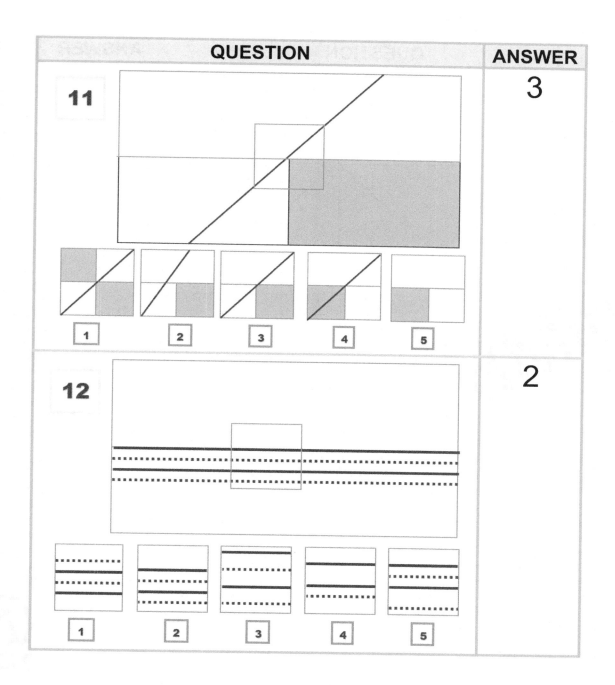

3

12

2

QUESTION	ANSWER

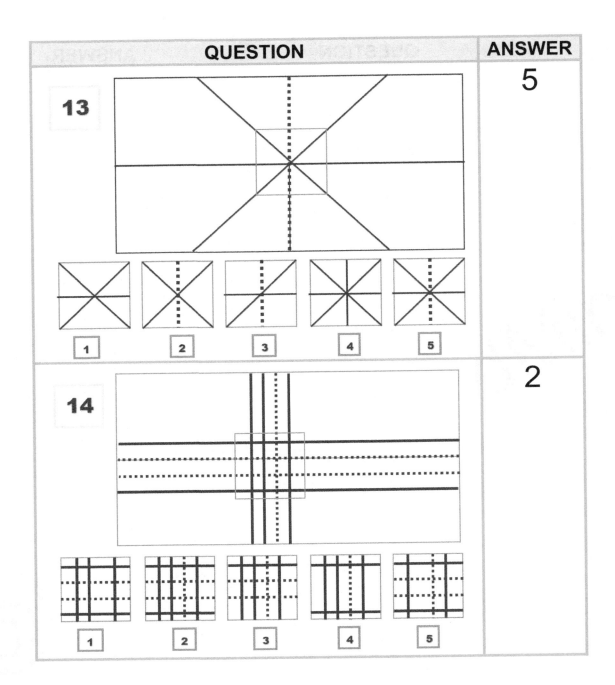

5

2

QUESTION	ANSWER
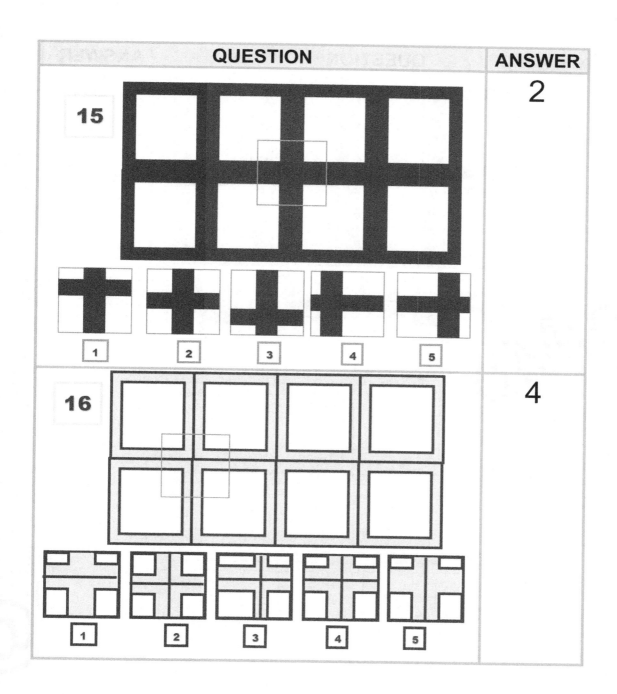	2
	4

QUESTION	ANSWER

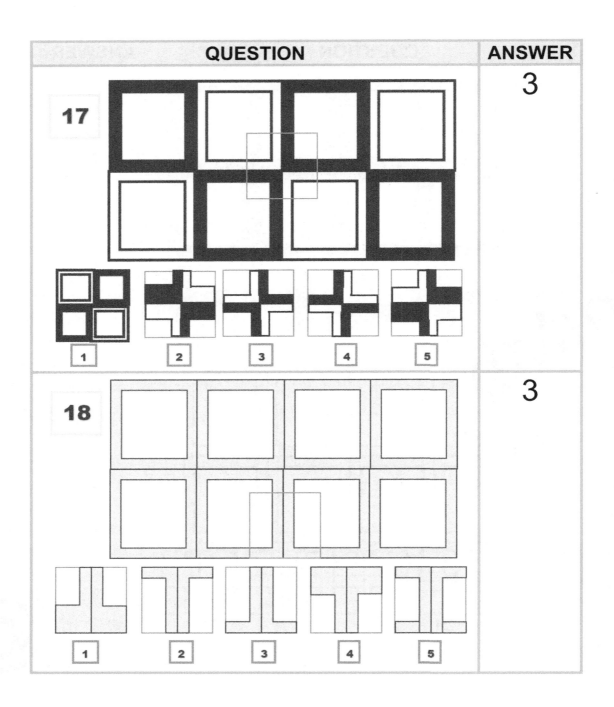

17 — ANSWER: 3

18 — ANSWER: 3

QUESTION	ANSWER
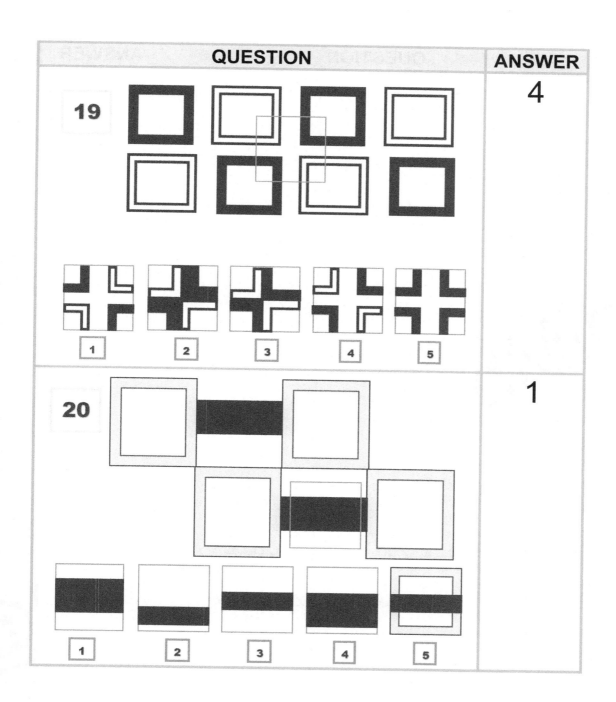	4
	1

QUESTION	ANSWER

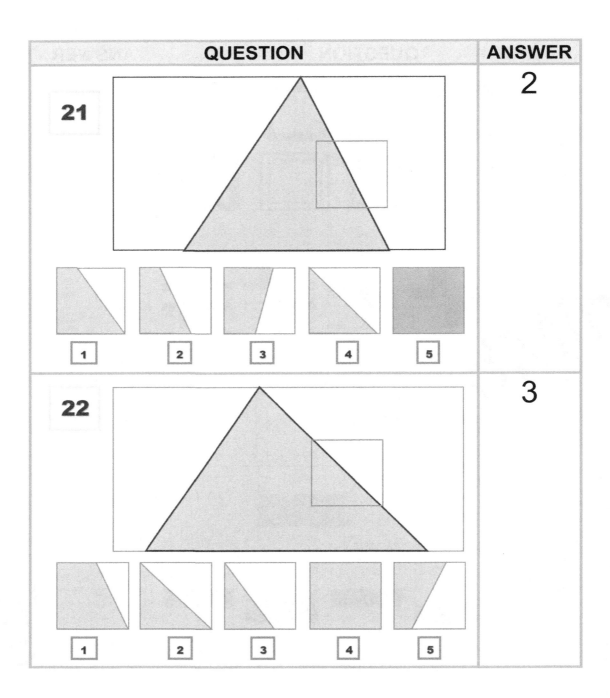

21

1   2   3   4   5

2

22

1   2   3   4   5

3

QUESTION	ANSWER

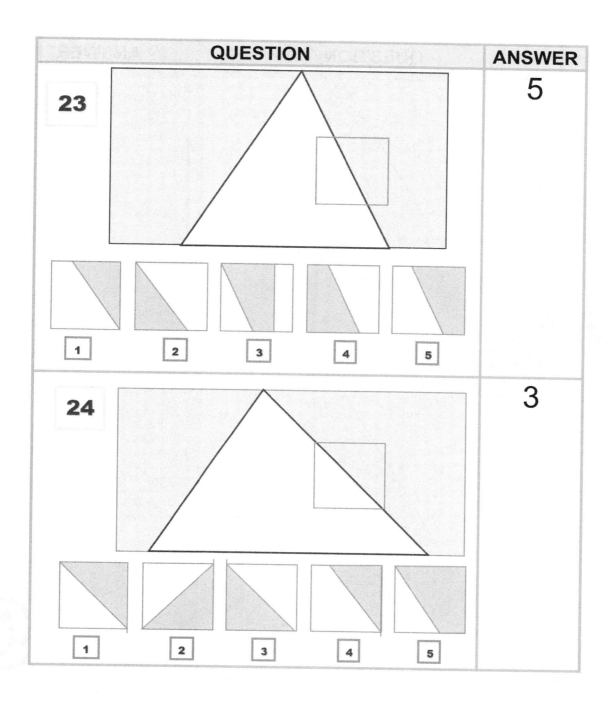

23

5

24

3

QUESTION	ANSWER
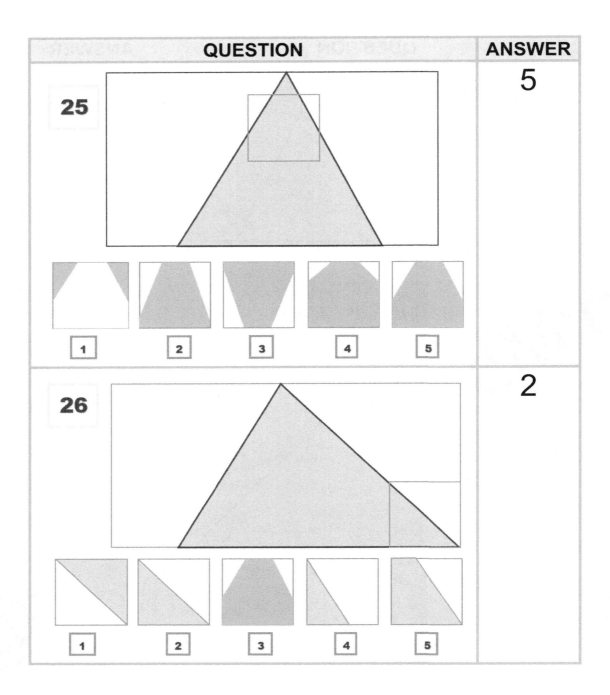	5
	2

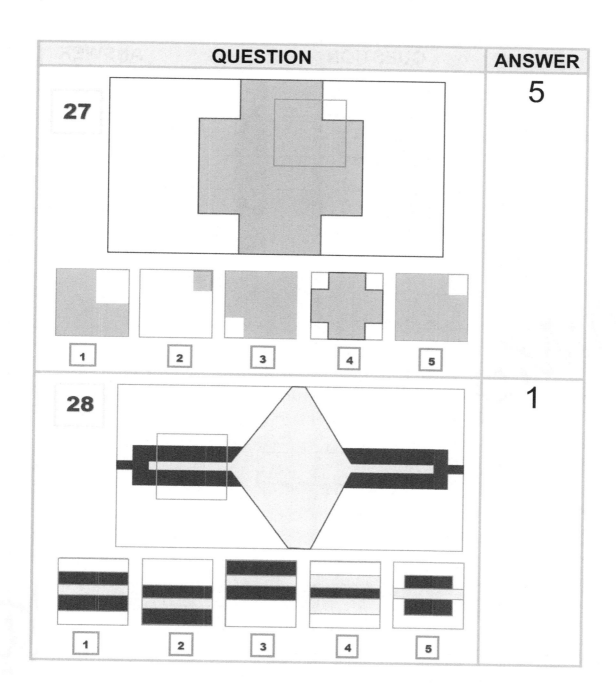

QUESTION	ANSWER
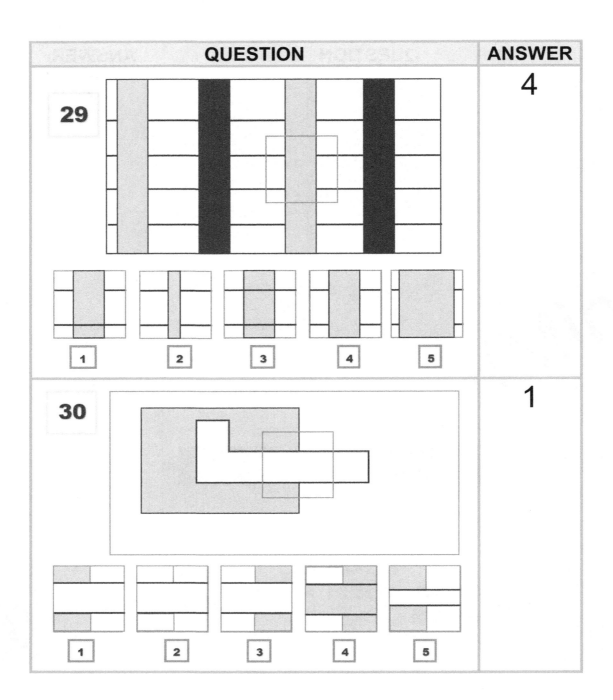	4
	1

QUESTION	ANSWER
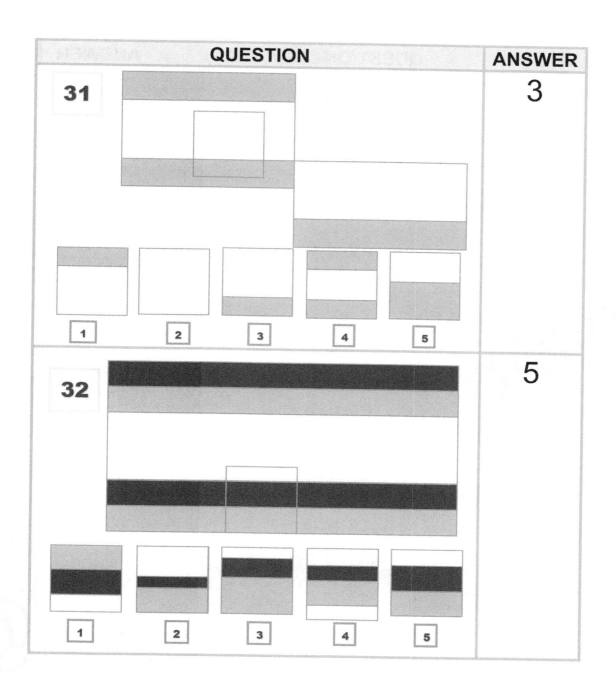	3
	5

QUESTION	ANSWER
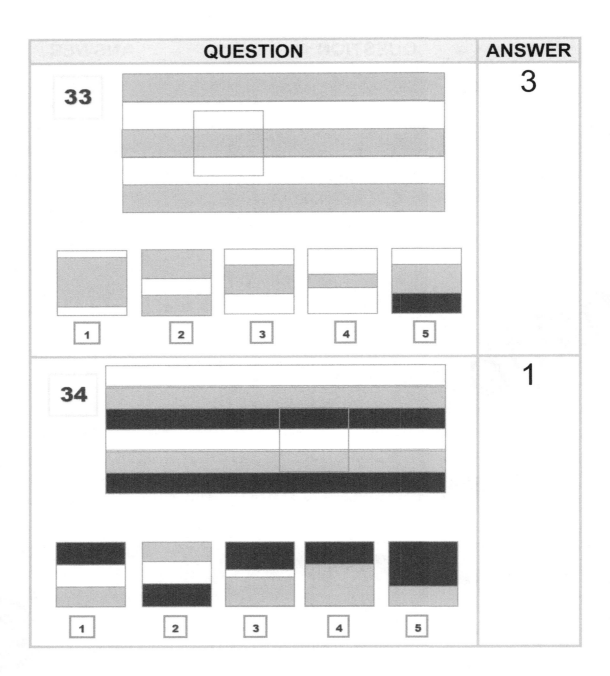	3
	1

QUESTION	ANSWER
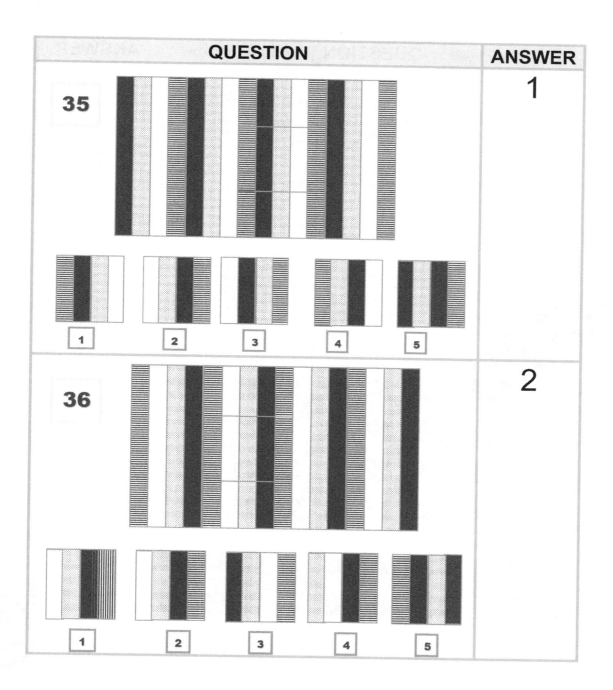	1
	2

195

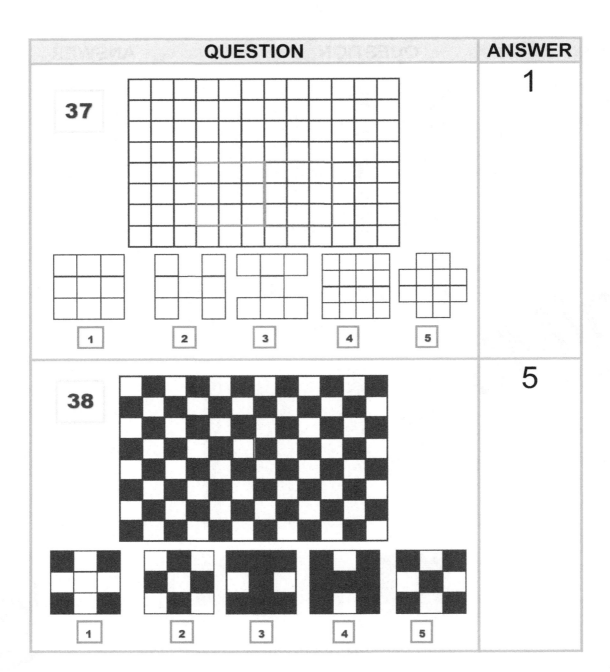

QUESTION	ANSWER

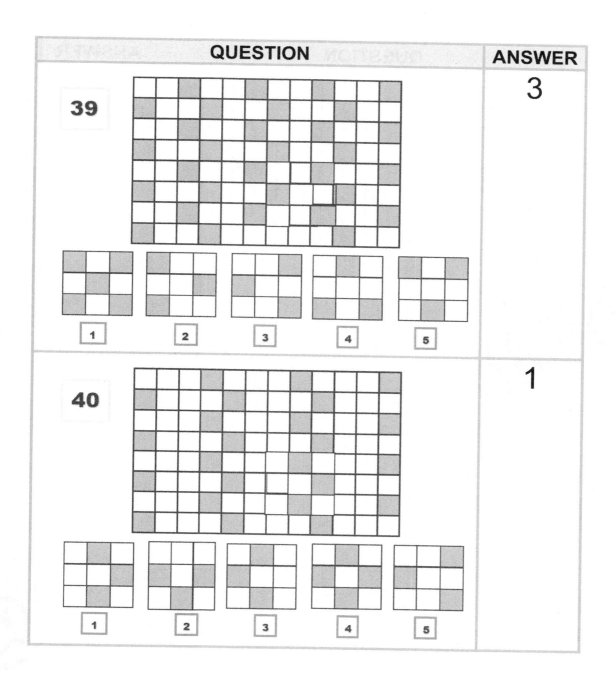

39 — 3

40 — 1

QUESTION	ANSWER
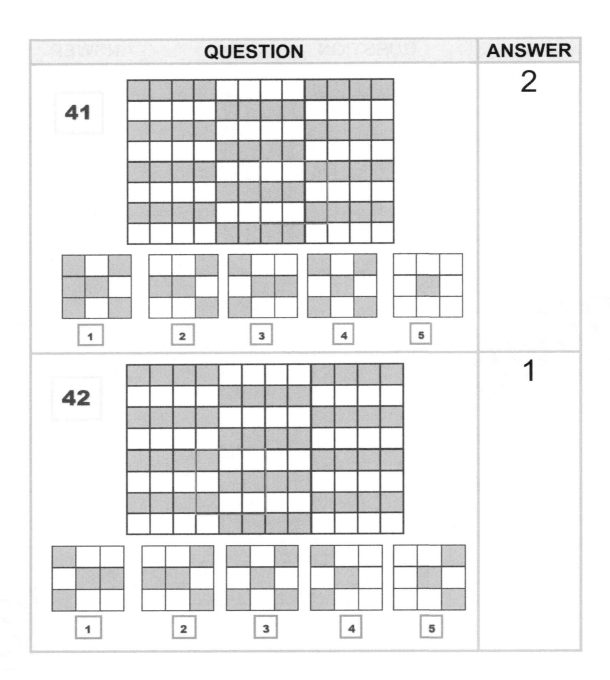	2
	1

198

QUESTION	ANSWER
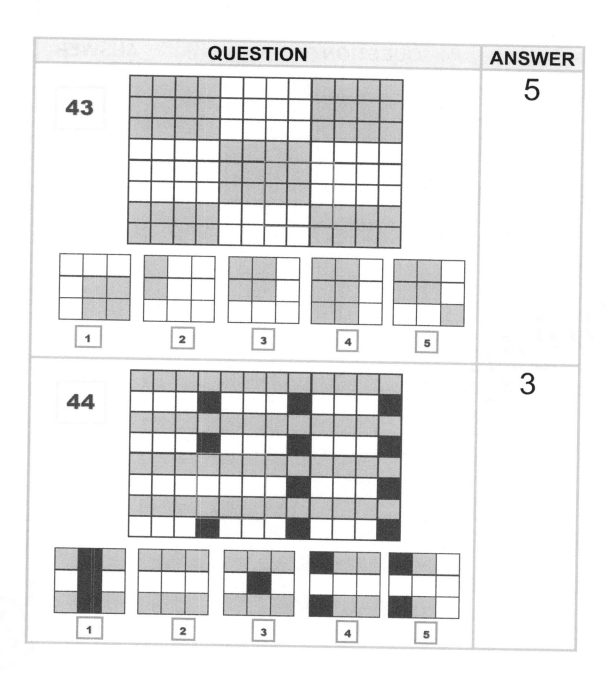	5
	3

QUESTION	ANSWER
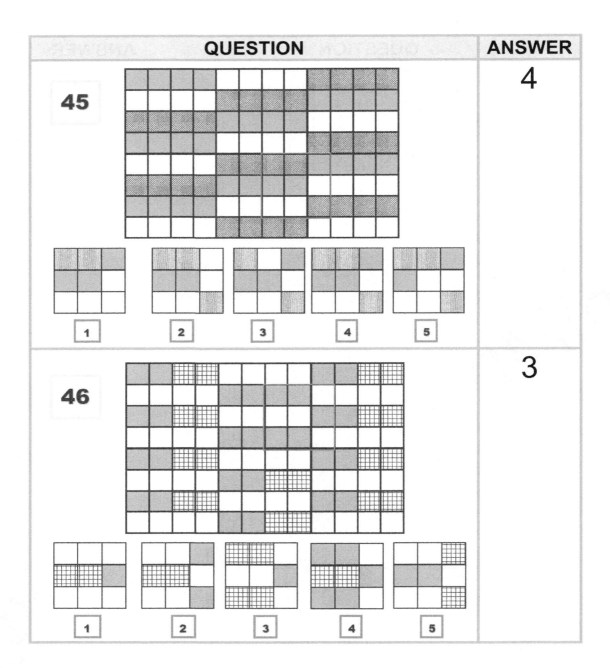	4
	3

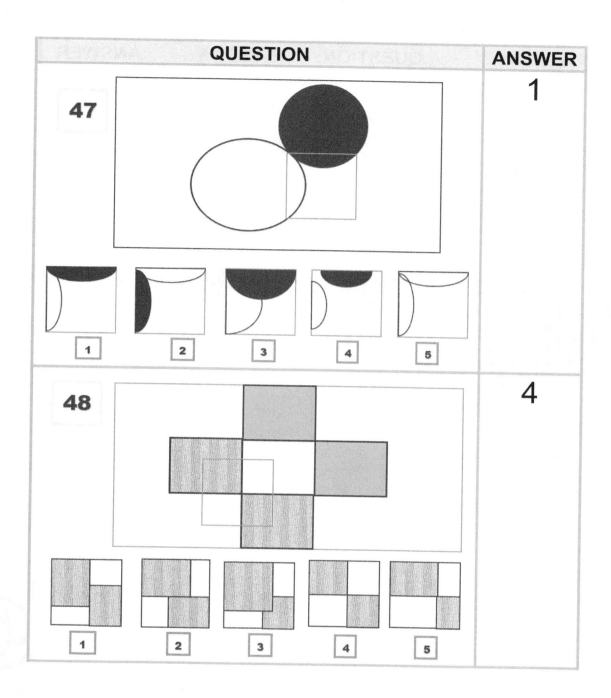

201

QUESTION	ANSWER

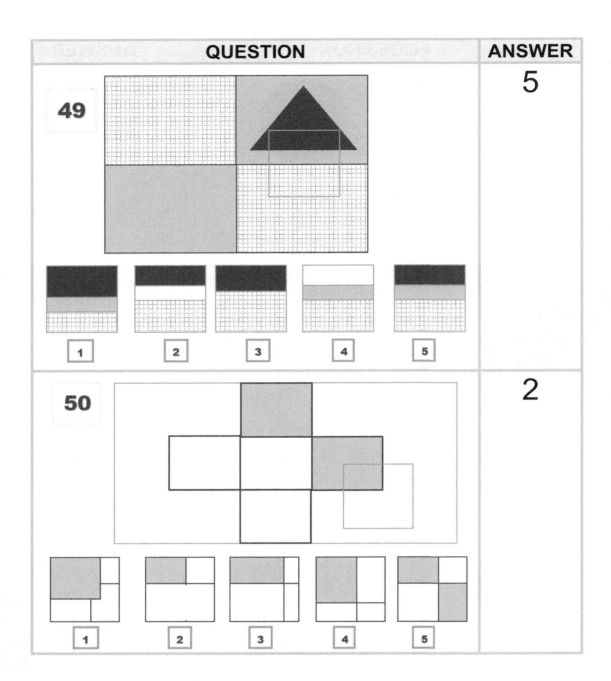

	5
	2

QUESTION	ANSWER
	2

51

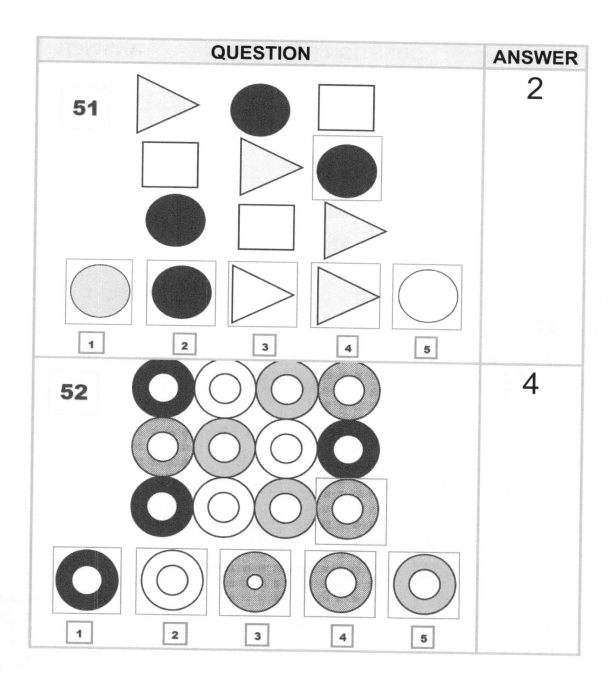

	4

52

QUESTION	ANSWER
	3
	5

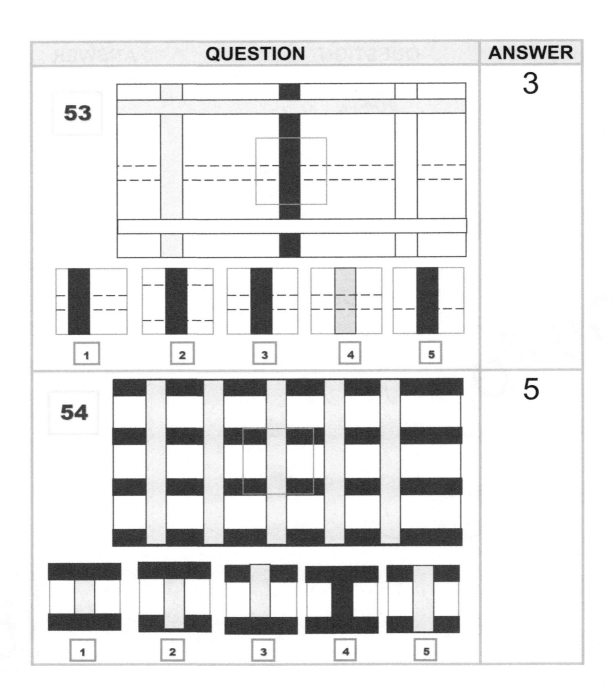

QUESTION	ANSWER
55 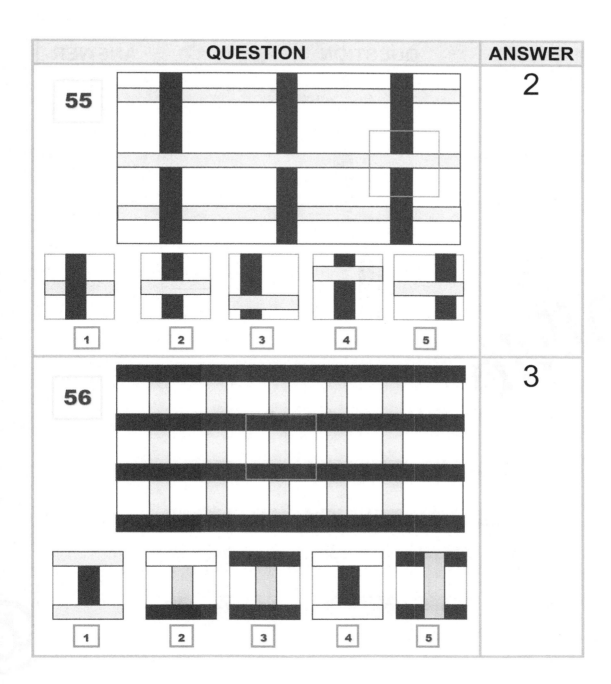	2
56	3

QUESTION	ANSWER
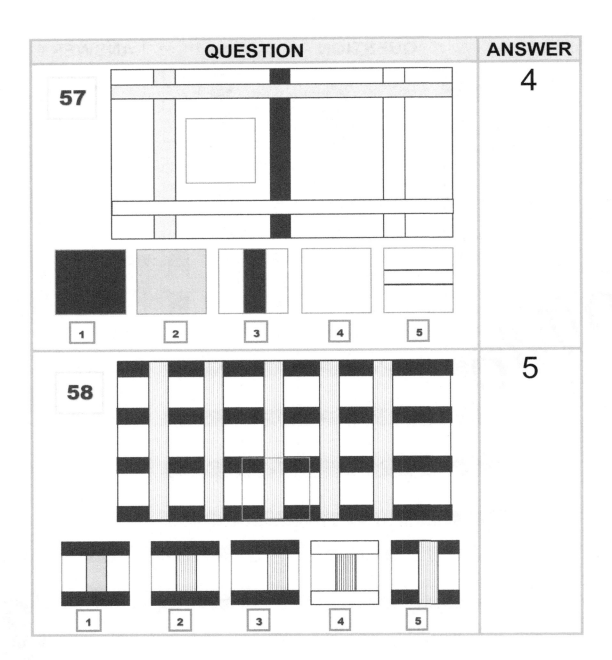	4
	5

QUESTION	ANSWER
59 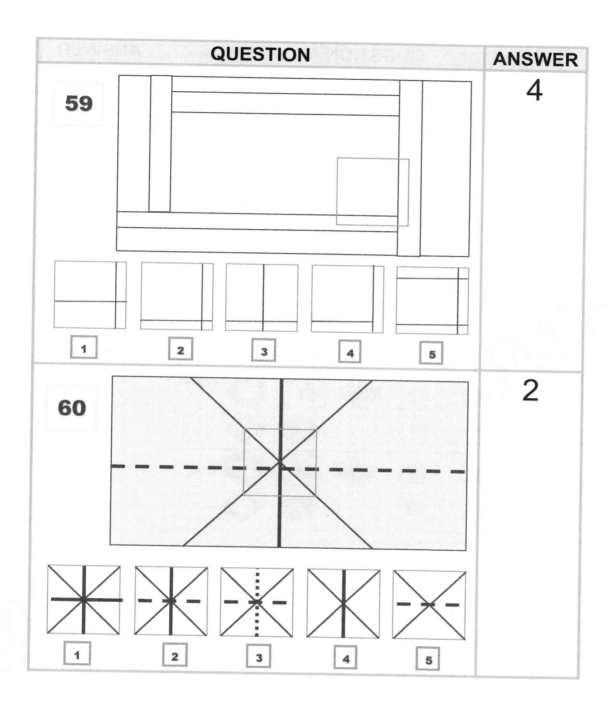	4
60	2

QUESTION	ANSWER

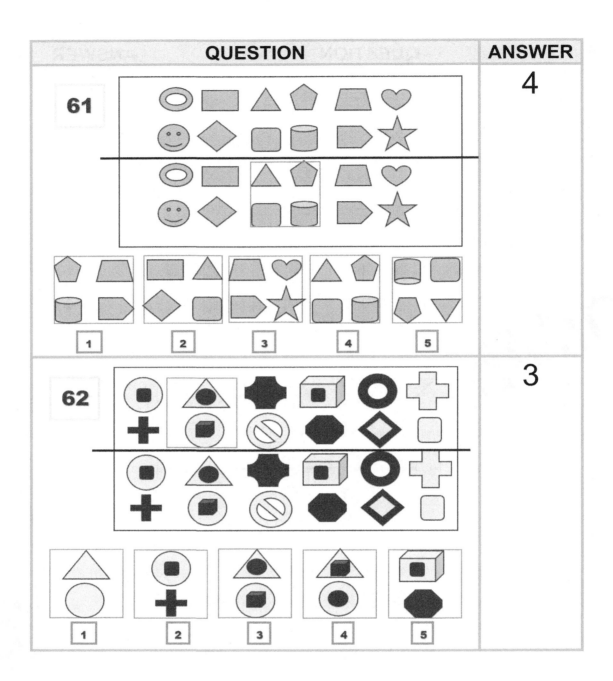

61 — Answer: **4**

62 — Answer: **3**

QUESTION	ANSWER
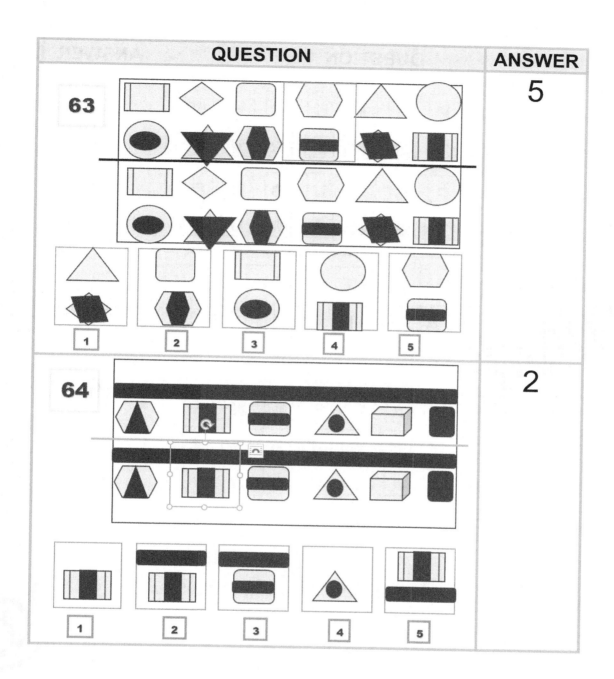 **63**	5
	2

QUESTION	ANSWER

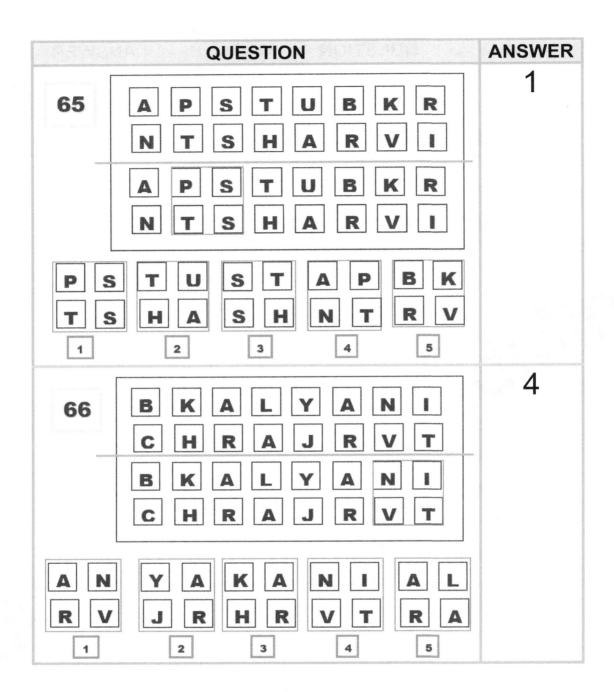

65

A	P	S	T	U	B	K	R
N	T	S	H	A	R	V	I

A	P	S	T	U	B	K	R
N	T	S	H	A	R	V	I

1	2	3	4	5
P S / T S	T U / H A	S T / S H	A P / N T	B K / R V

Answer: 1

66

B	K	A	L	Y	A	N	I
C	H	R	A	J	R	V	T

B	K	A	L	Y	A	N	I
C	H	R	A	J	R	V	T

1	2	3	4	5
A N / R V	Y A / J R	K A / H R	N I / V T	A L / R A

Answer: 4

210

QUESTION	ANSWER
67	**3**

Row 1: 2 5 V 3 9 T G 6
Row 2: C 1 X 7 5 4 P 8

Row 1: 2 5 V 3 9 T G 6
Row 2: C 1 X 7 5 4 P 8

Options:
1. V 3 / X 7
2. V 3 / X 7
3. 9 T / 5 4
4. T G / 4 P
5. G 6 / P 8

QUESTION	ANSWER
68	**5**

Row 1: 1 8 7 4 3 2 5 9
Row 2: 3 6 4 1 9 7 8 2

Row 1: 1 8 7 4 3 2 5 9
Row 2: 3 6 4 1 9 7 8 2

Options:
1. 1 8 / 3 6
2. 7 4 / 4 1
3. 1 9 / 4 3
4. 2 5 / 7 8
5. 8 7 / 6 4

QUESTION	ANSWER
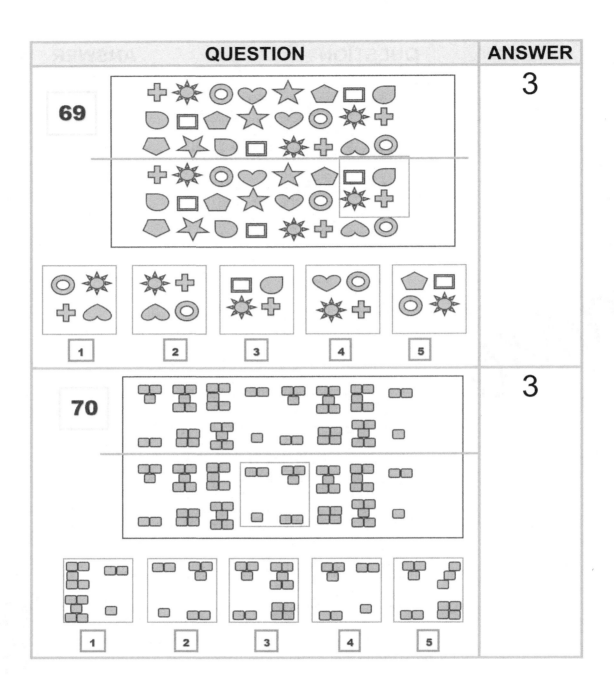	3
	3

QUESTION	ANSWER

71

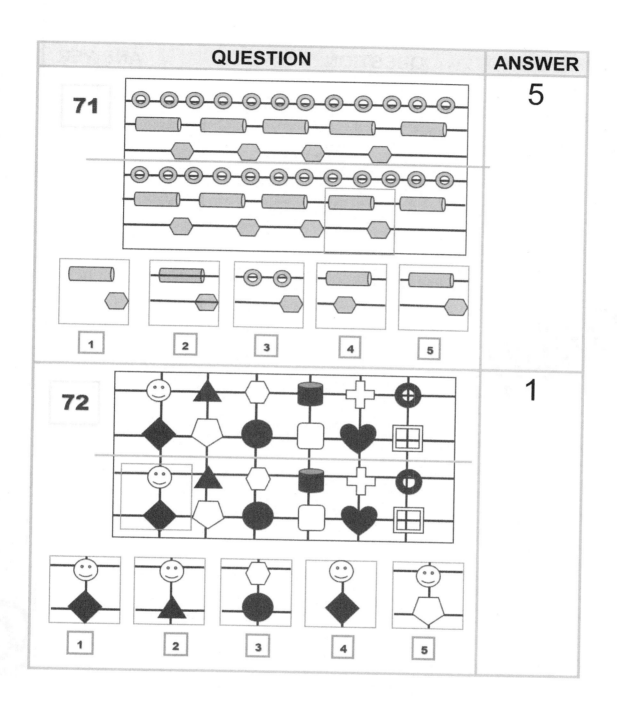

5

72

1

QUESTION	ANSWER
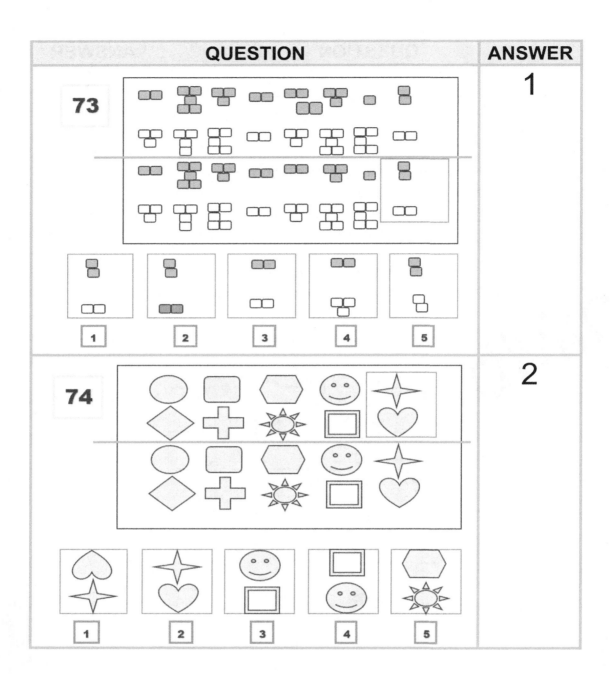	1
	2

214

QUESTION	ANSWER
75 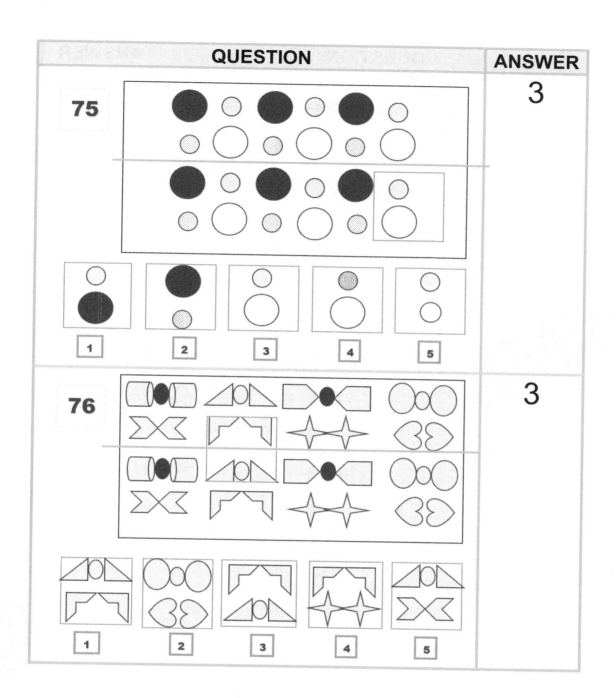	3
76	3

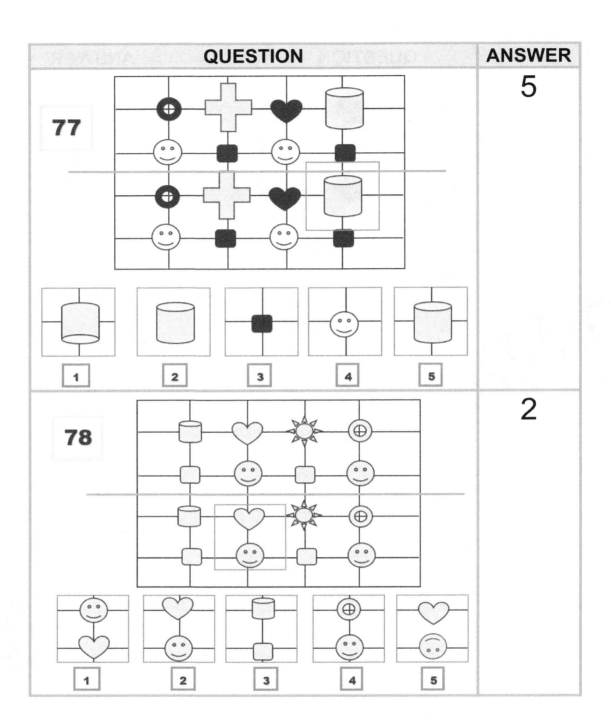

216

QUESTION	ANSWER

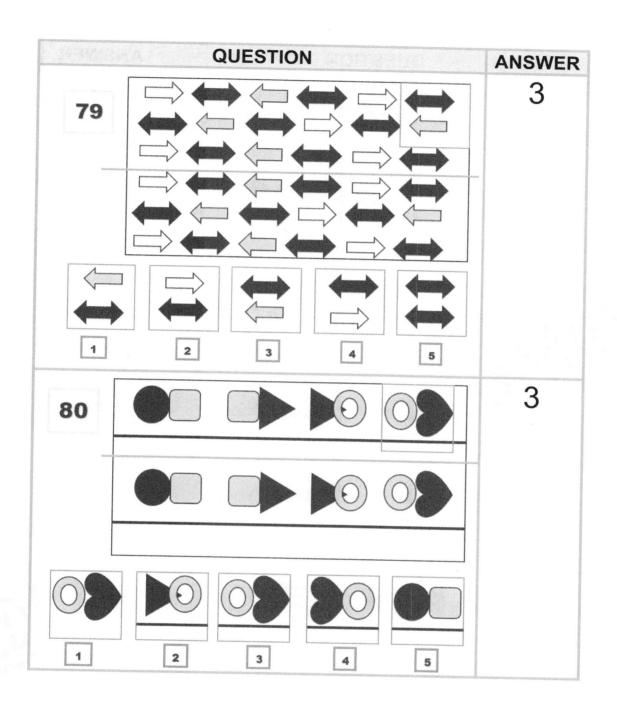

79 → 3

80 → 3

QUESTION	ANSWER
	3

81

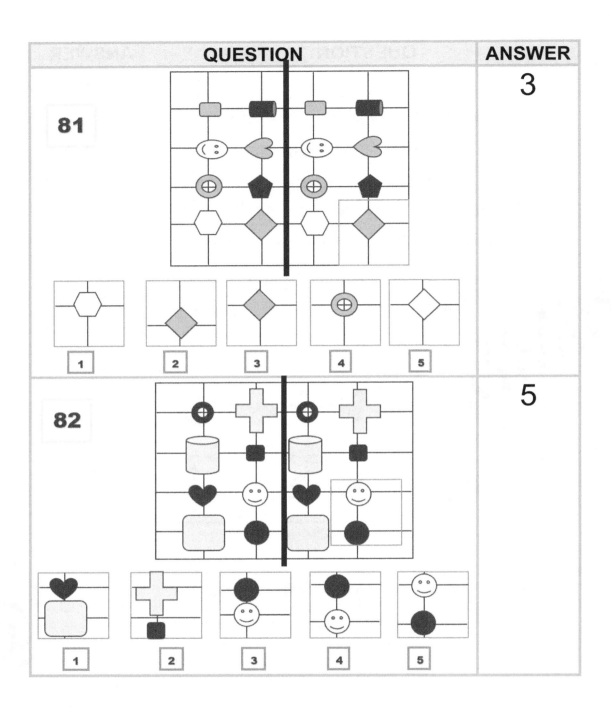

1	2	3	4	5

82

	5

1	2	3	4	5

QUESTION	ANSWER
83 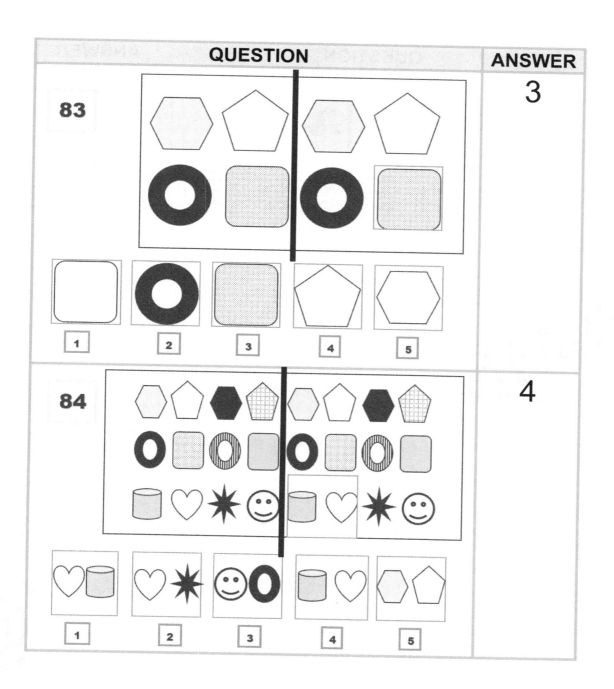	3
84	4

QUESTION	ANSWER

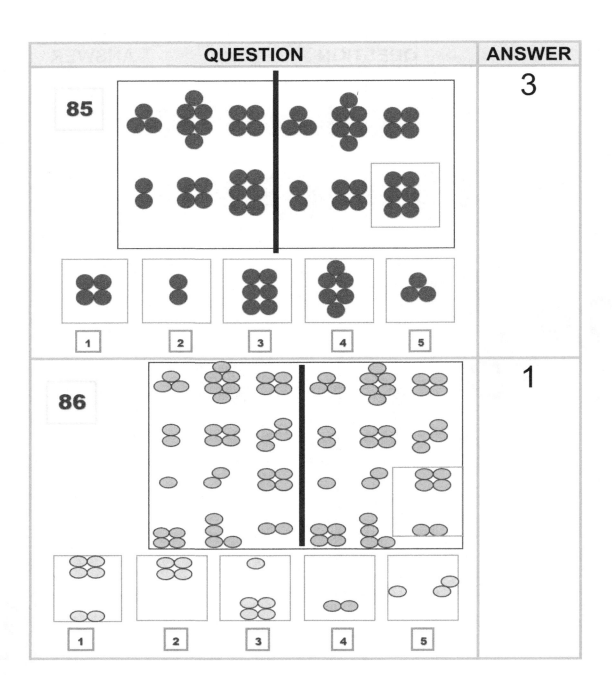

85 — Answer: **3**

86 — Answer: **1**

QUESTION	ANSWER
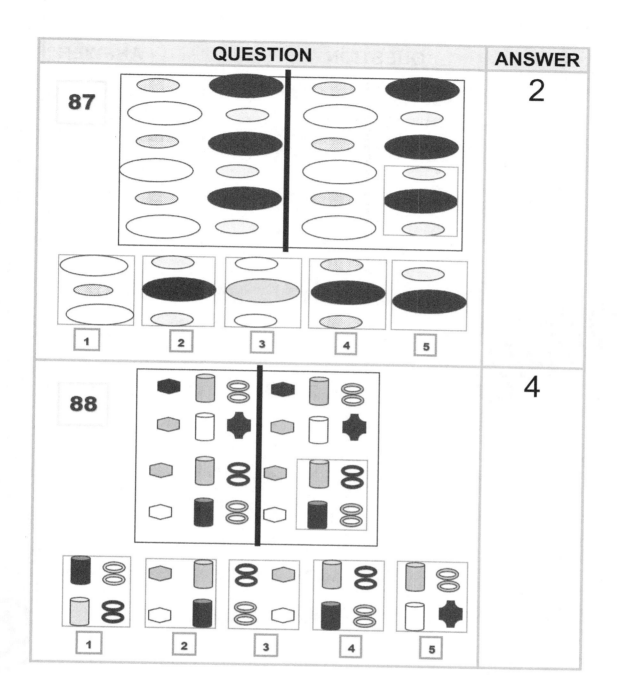	2
	4

QUESTION	ANSWER
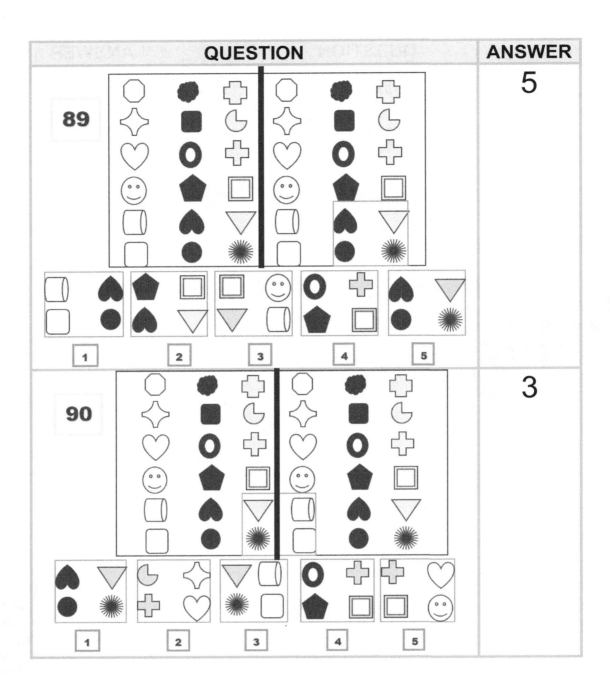	5
	3

QUESTION	ANSWER
91 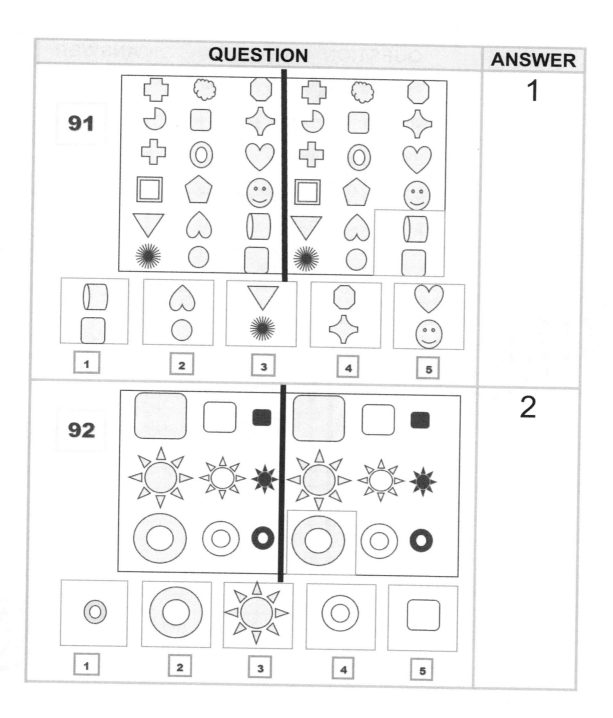	**1**
92	**2**

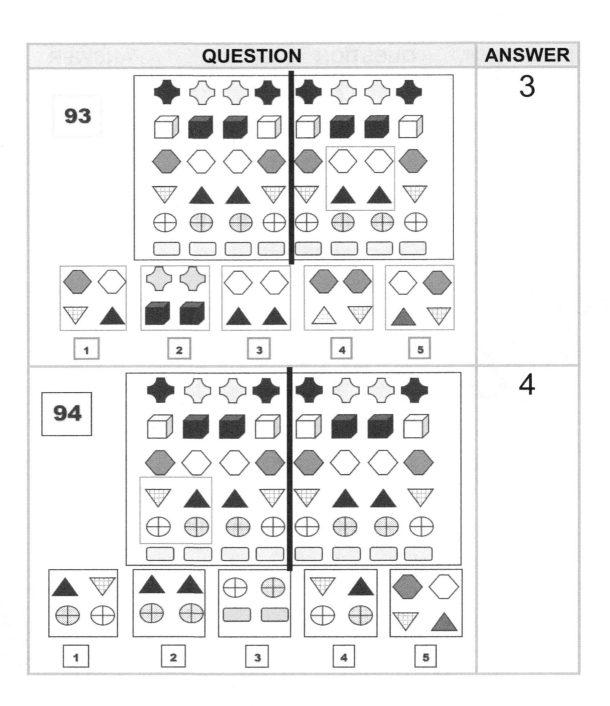

QUESTION	ANSWER
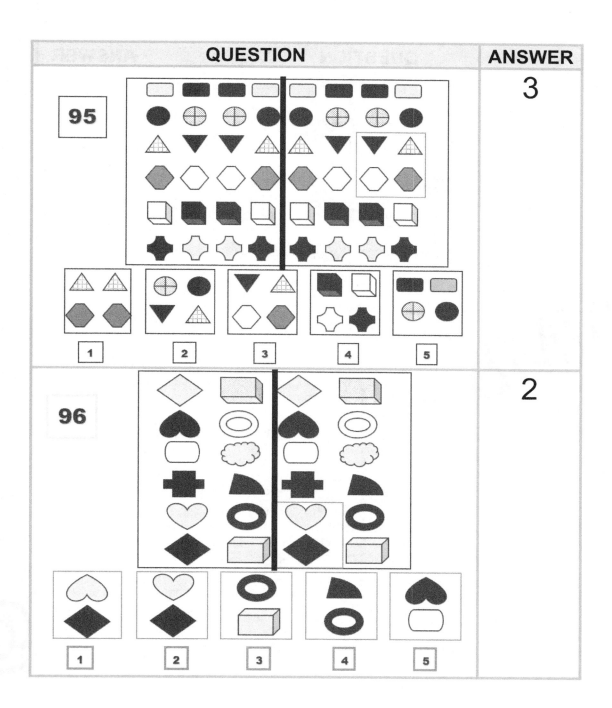	3
	2

QUESTION	ANSWER
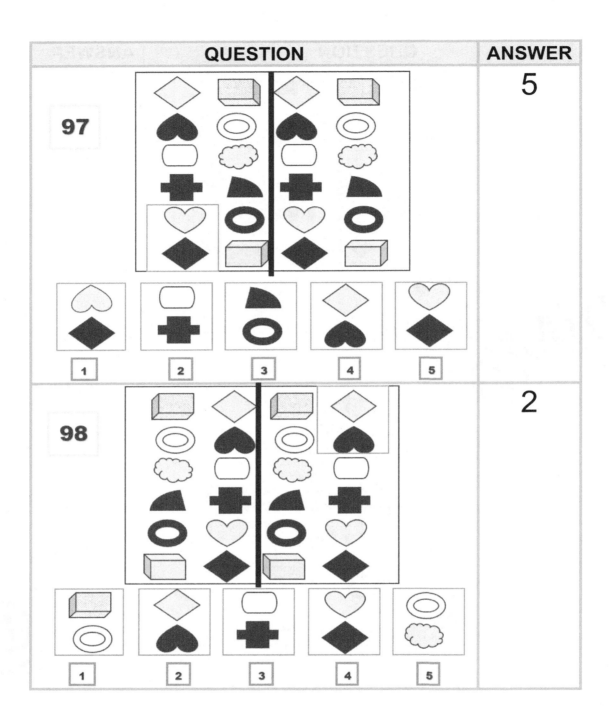 **97**	5
98	2

QUESTION	ANSWER
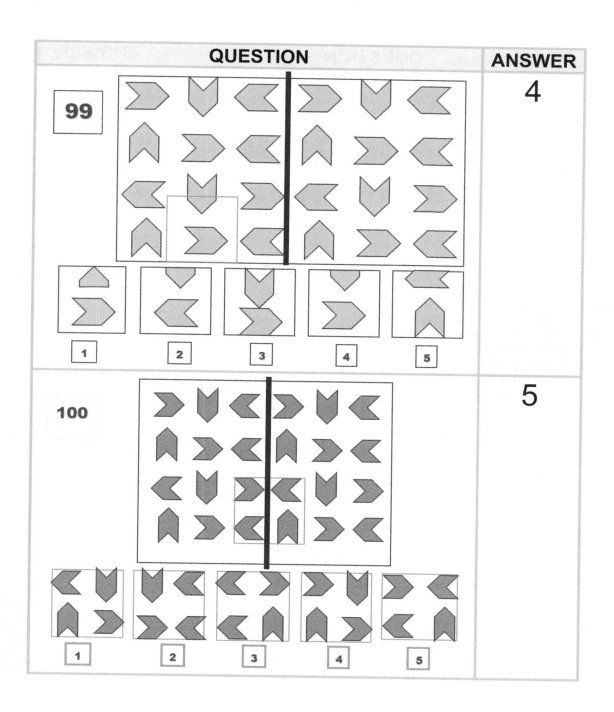 **99**	4
100	5

QUESTION	ANSWER

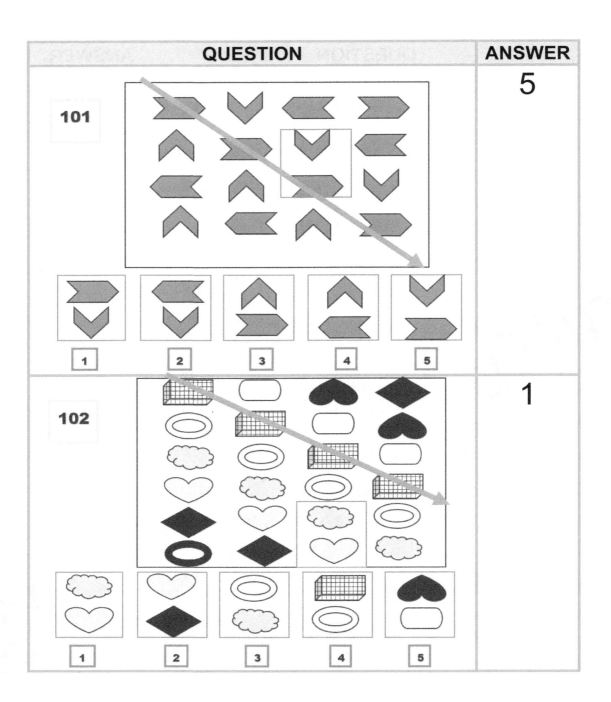

101 — **5**

102 — **1**

QUESTION	ANSWER

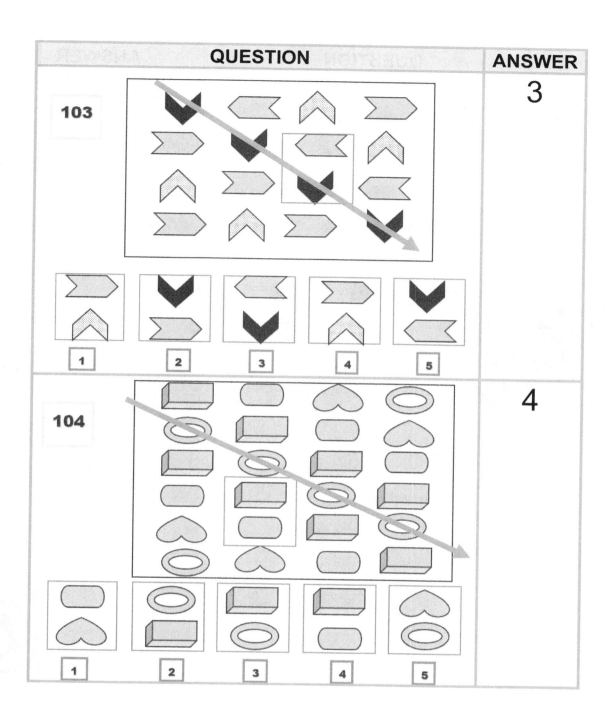

103 — **3**

104 — **4**

QUESTION	ANSWER
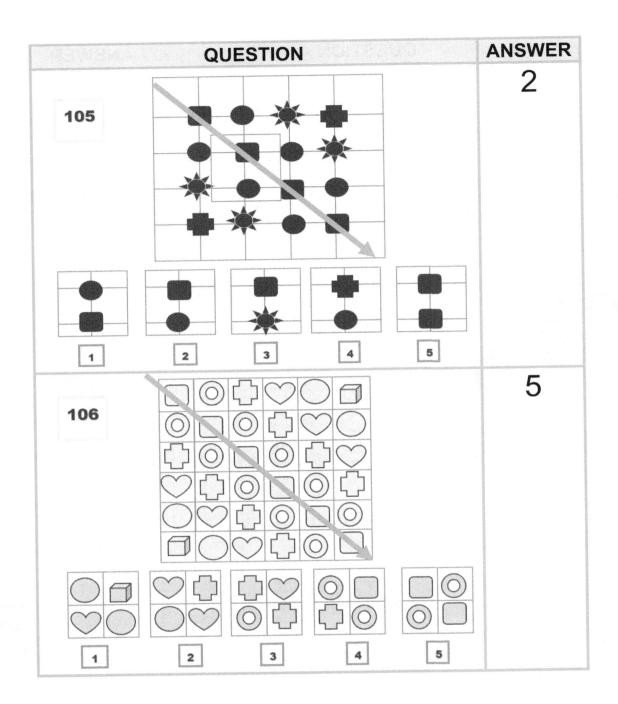	2
	5

QUESTION	ANSWER
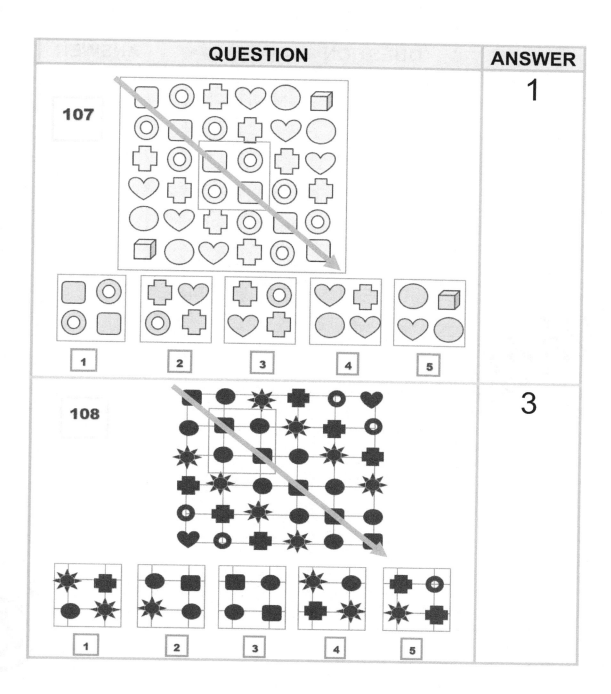	1
	3

QUESTION	ANSWER
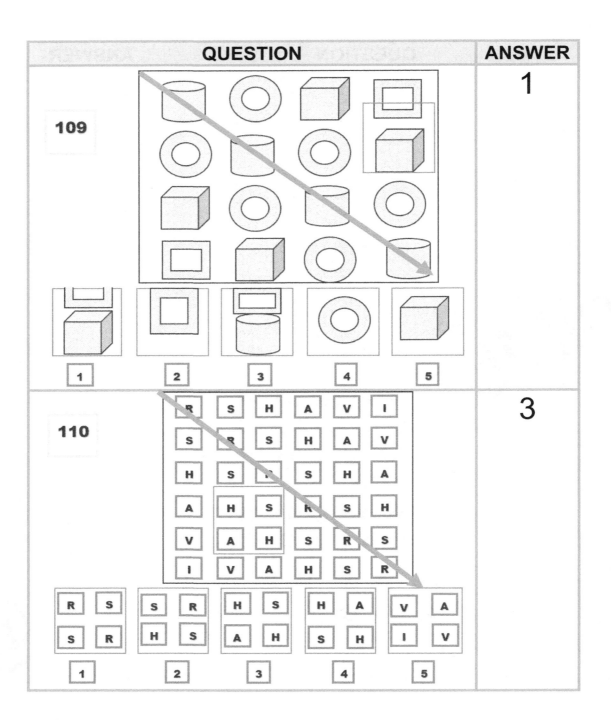	1
	3

QUESTION	ANSWER

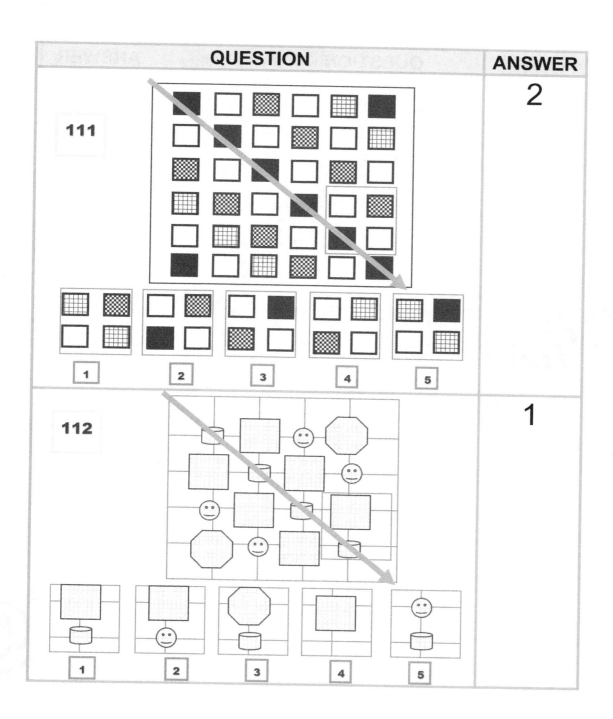

111

2

112

1

233

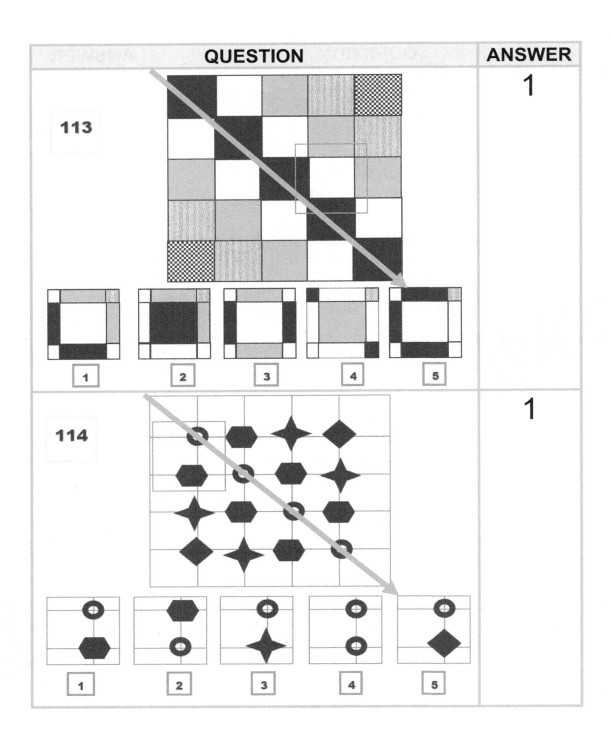

QUESTION	ANSWER
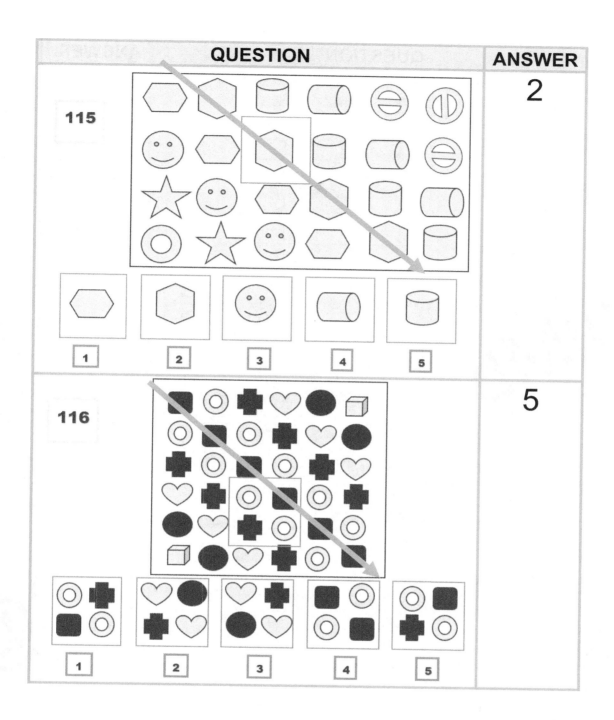	2
	5

QUESTION	ANSWER
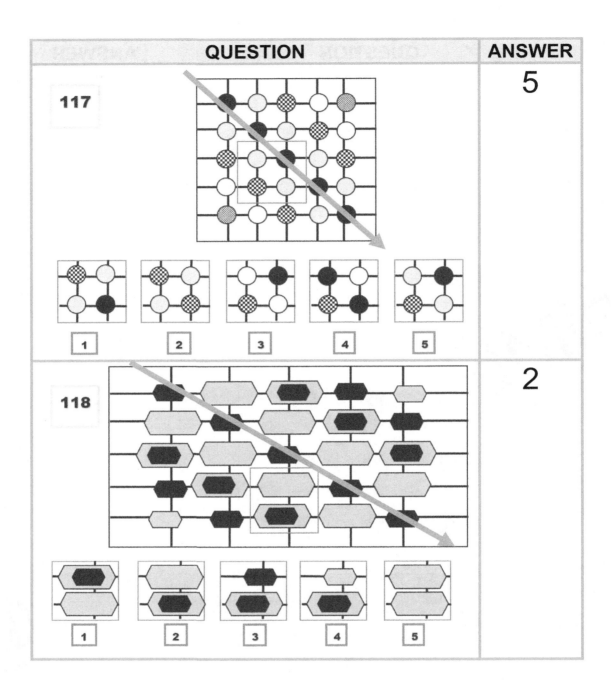	5
	2

QUESTION	ANSWER

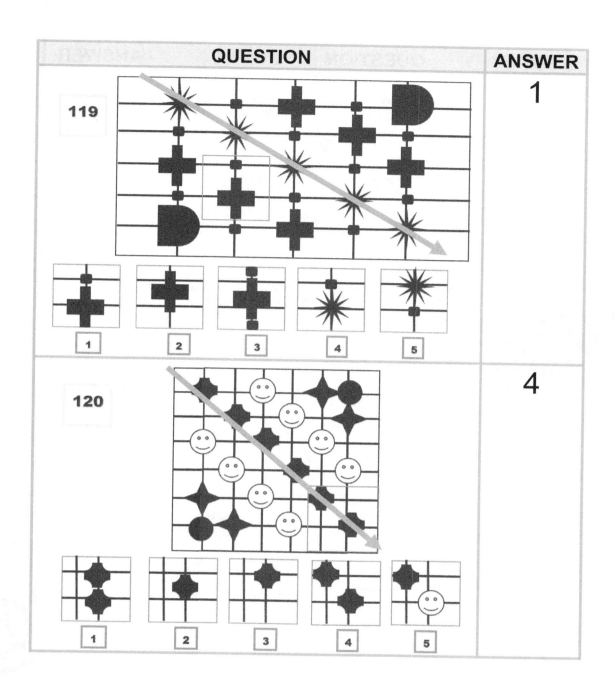

119	**1**
120	**4**

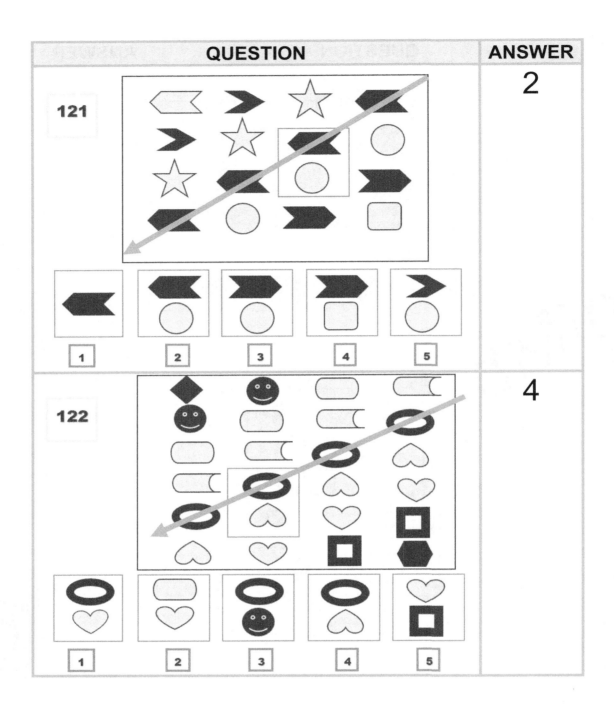

	ANSWER
121	2
122	4

QUESTION	ANSWER
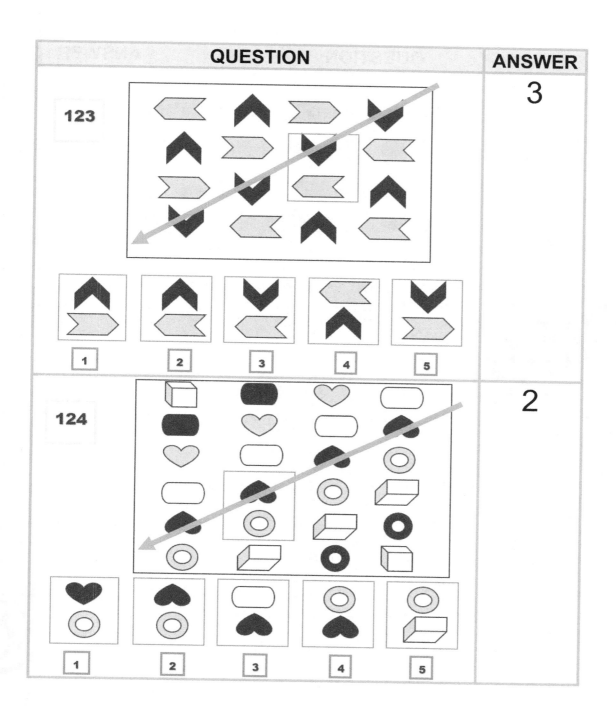	3
	2

QUESTION	ANSWER
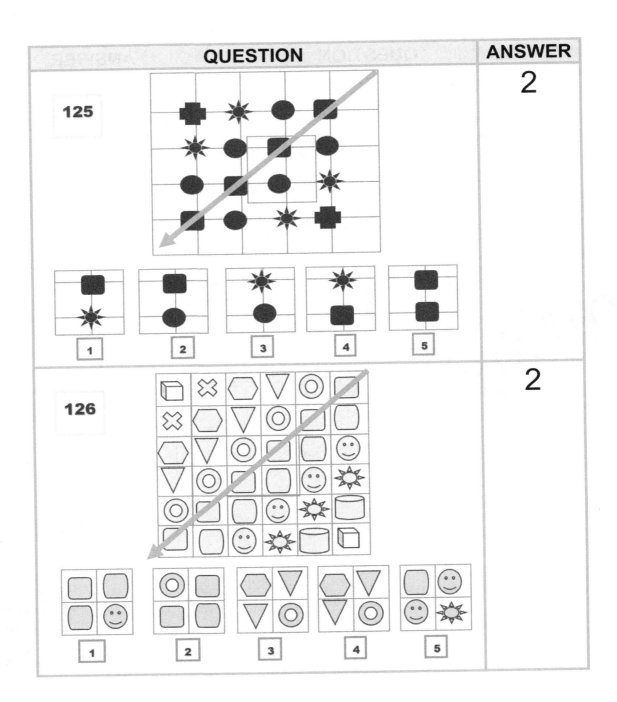	2
	2

QUESTION	ANSWER

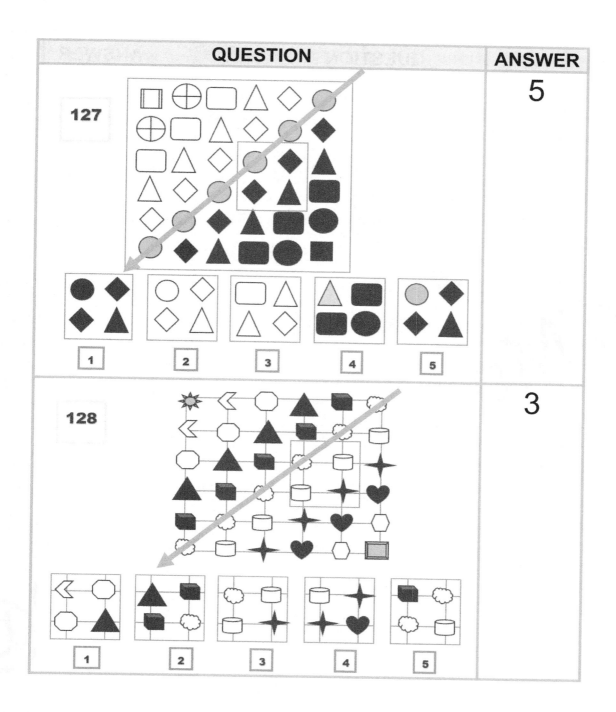

127

5

128

3

QUESTION	ANSWER

129

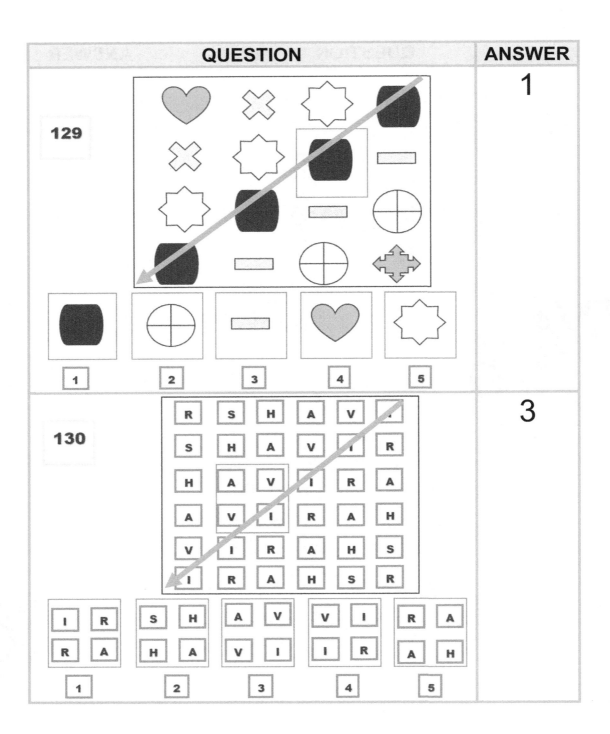

1

130

3

QUESTION	ANSWER
131 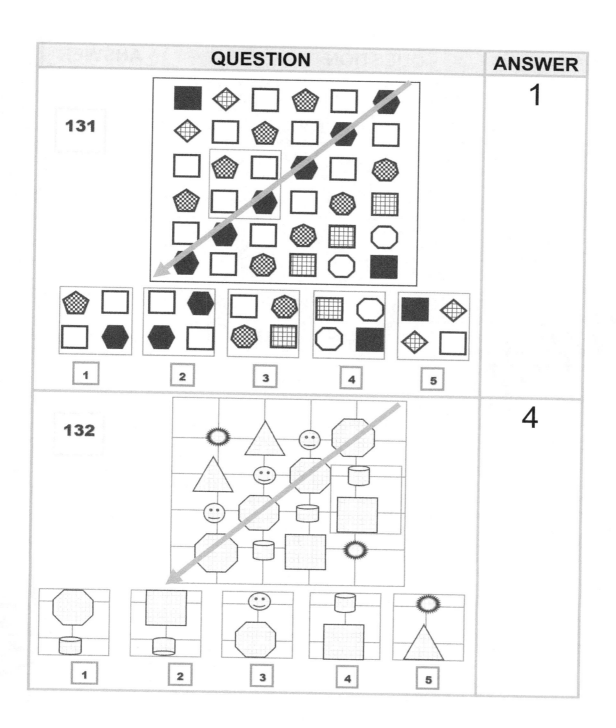	1
132	4

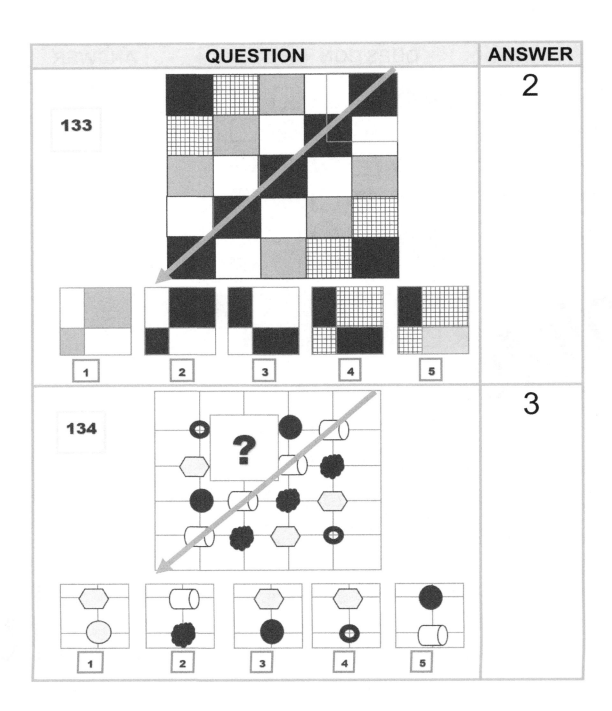

133	2
134	3

QUESTION	ANSWER
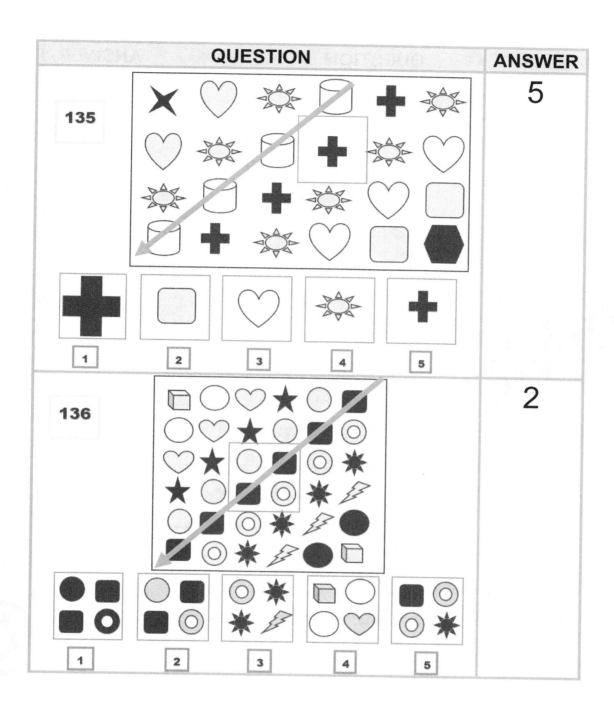	5
	2

QUESTION	ANSWER
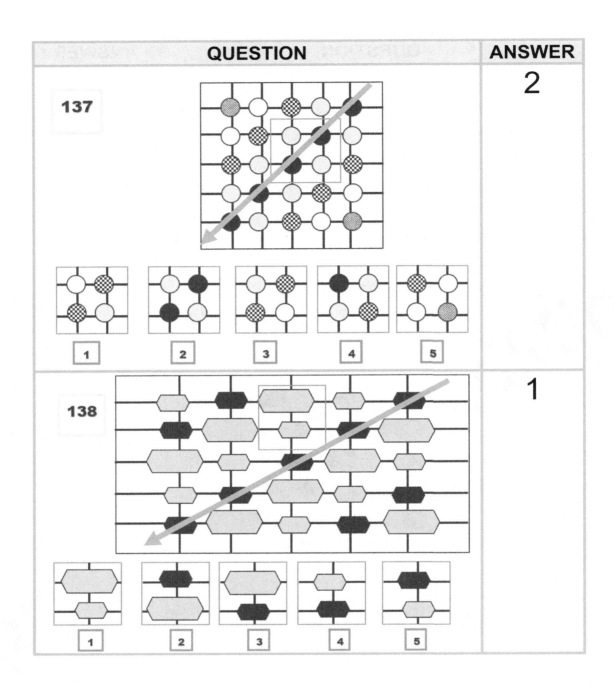	2
	1

QUESTION	ANSWER

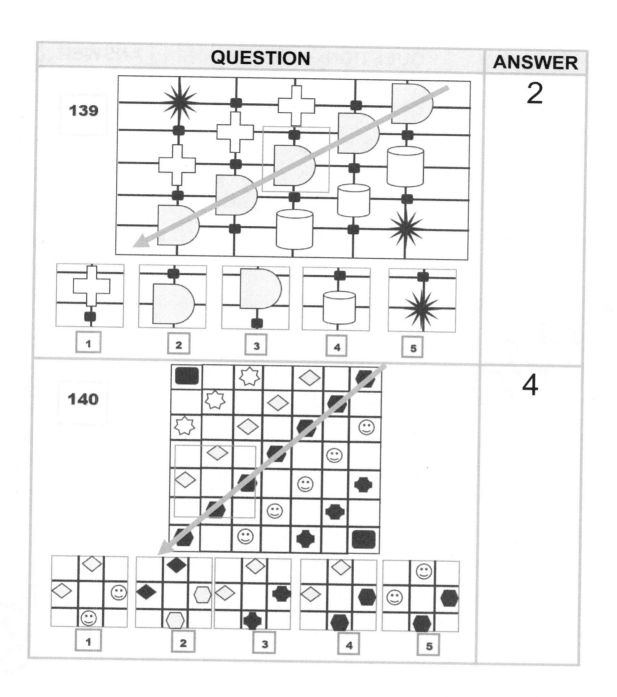

139 ... Answer: **2**

140 ... Answer: **4**

QUESTION	ANSWER
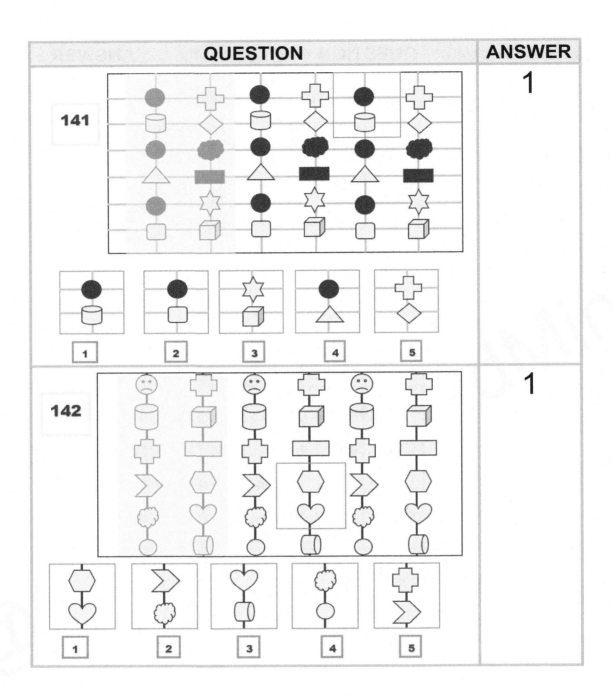	1
	1

QUESTION	ANSWER
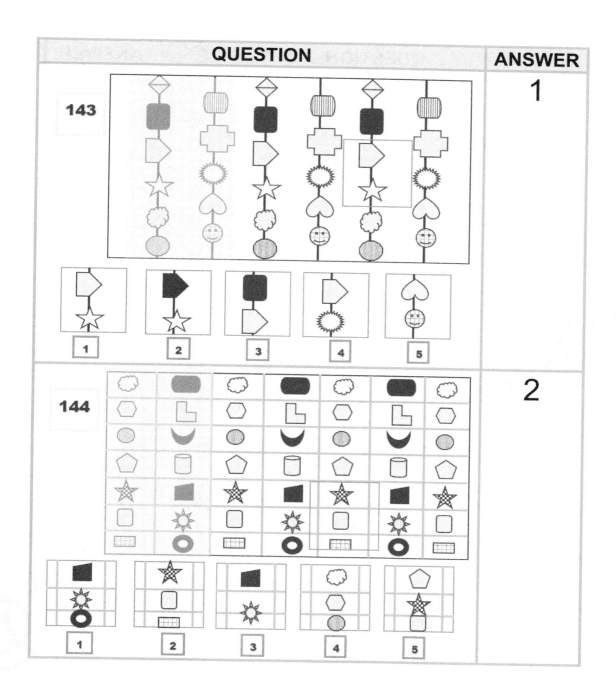	1
	2

QUESTION	ANSWER
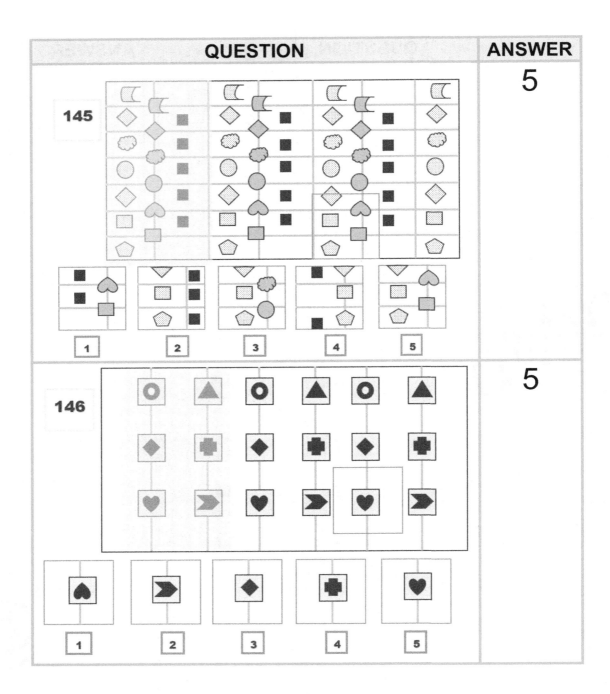	5
	5

QUESTION	ANSWER

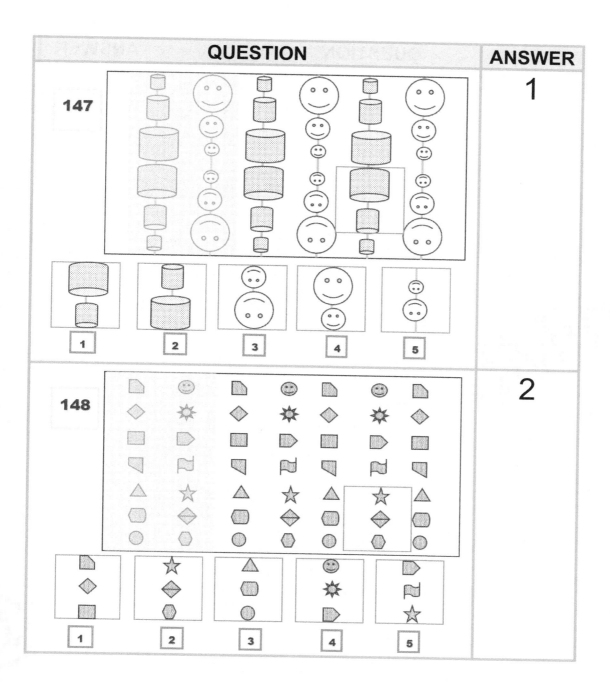

147 — Answer: **1**

148 — Answer: **2**

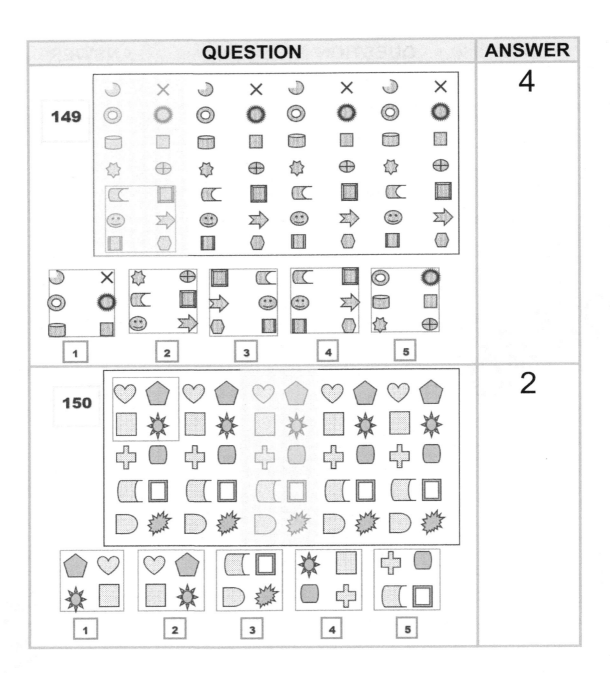

149	4
150	2

QUESTION	ANSWER

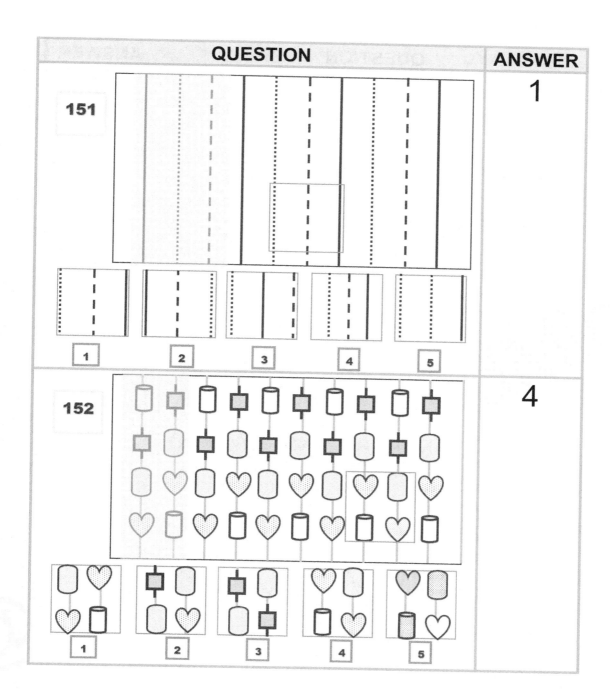

151 — Answer: 1

152 — Answer: 4

QUESTION	ANSWER
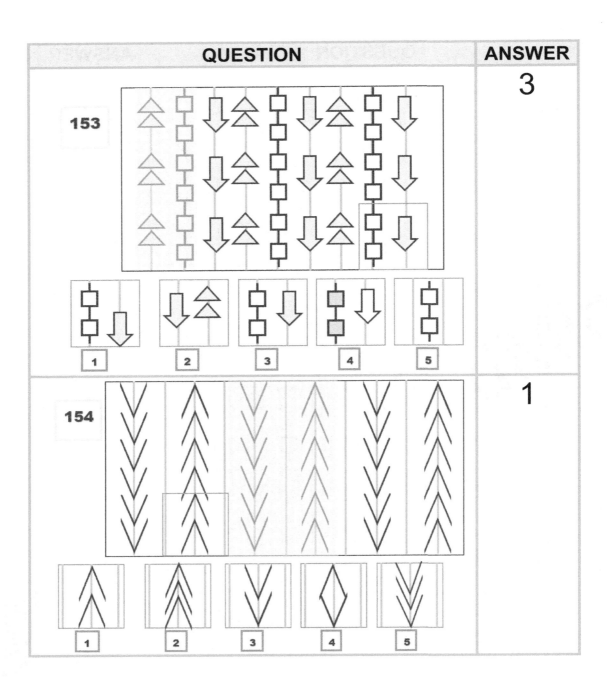	3
	1

QUESTION	ANSWER
155 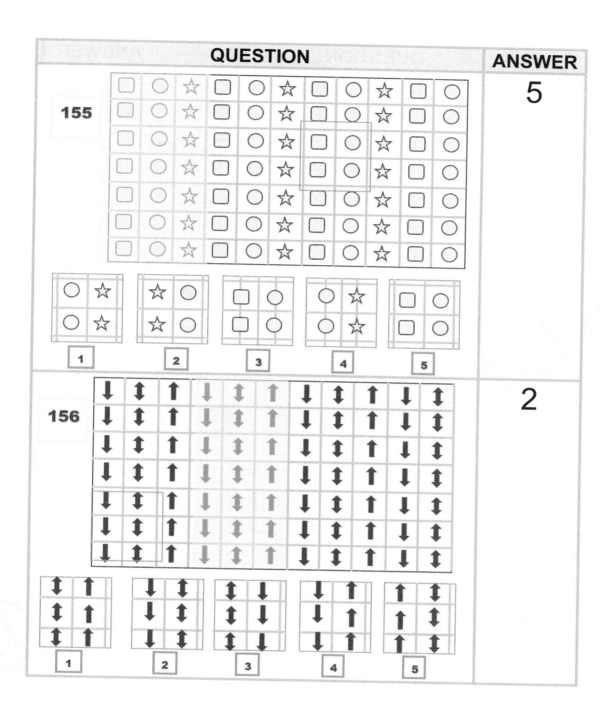	**5**
156	**2**

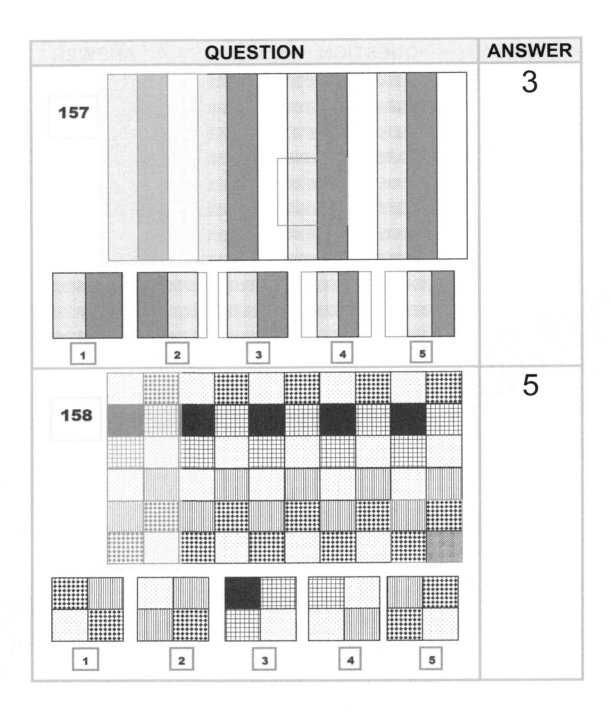

QUESTION	ANSWER
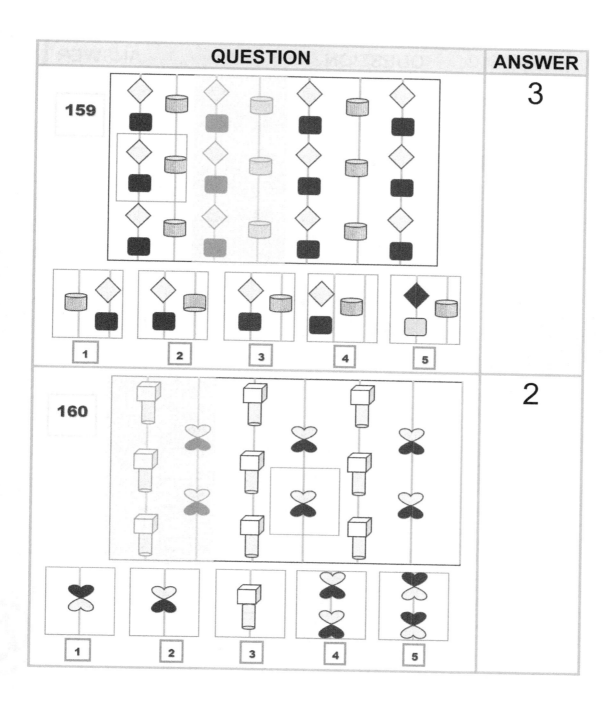	3
	2

QUESTION	ANSWER

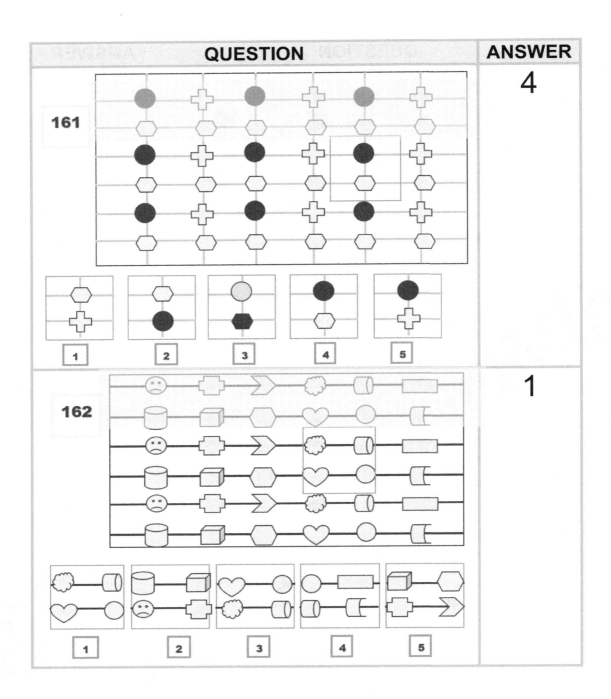

161   **4**

162   **1**

QUESTION	ANSWER
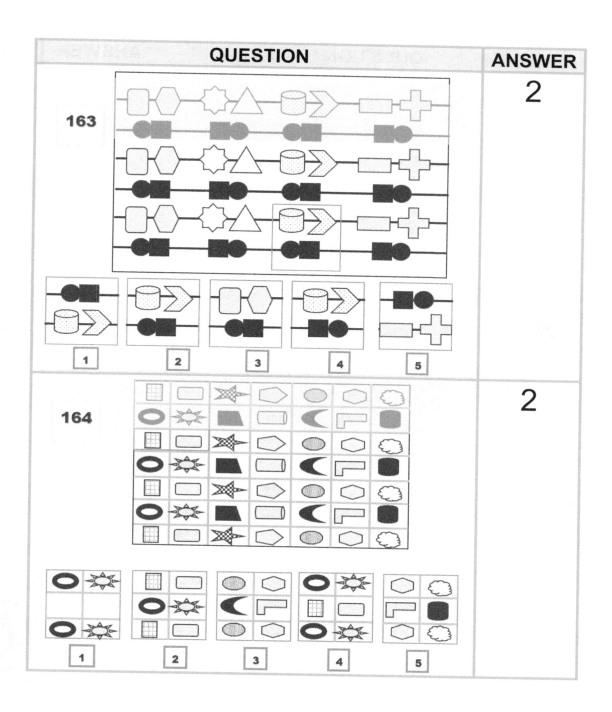	2
	2

QUESTION	ANSWER
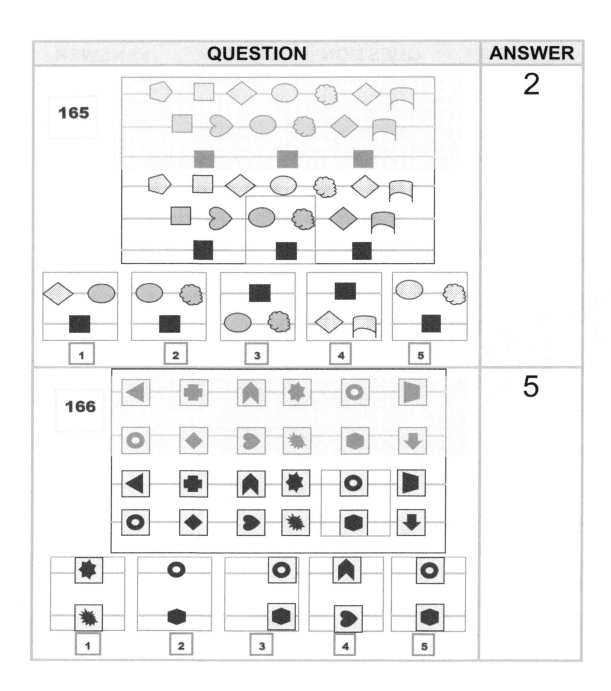	2
	5

QUESTION	ANSWER
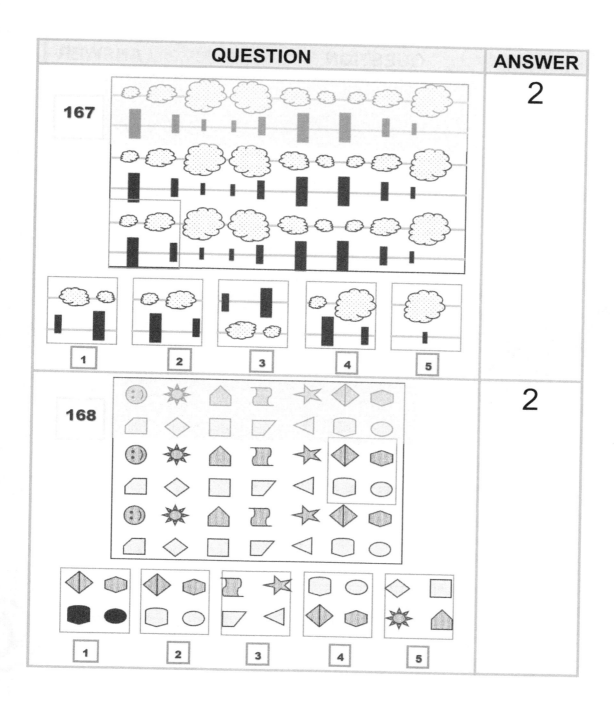	2
	2

QUESTION	ANSWER

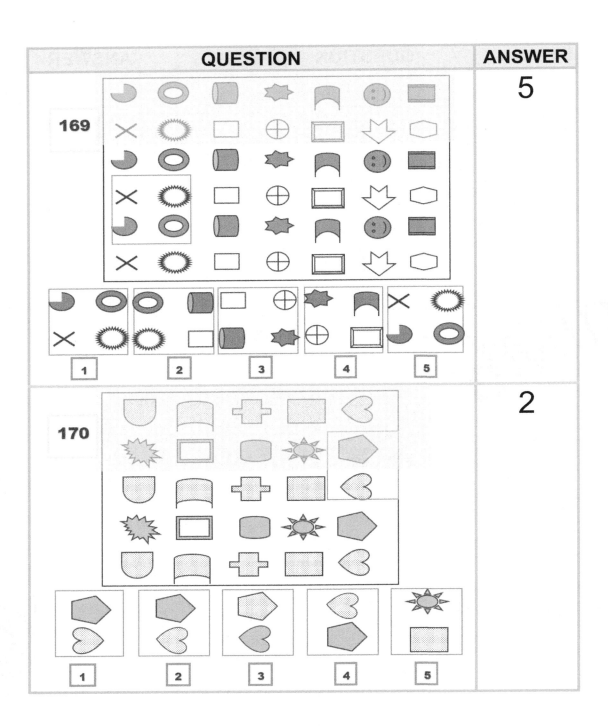

	5
169	
170	2

QUESTION	ANSWER

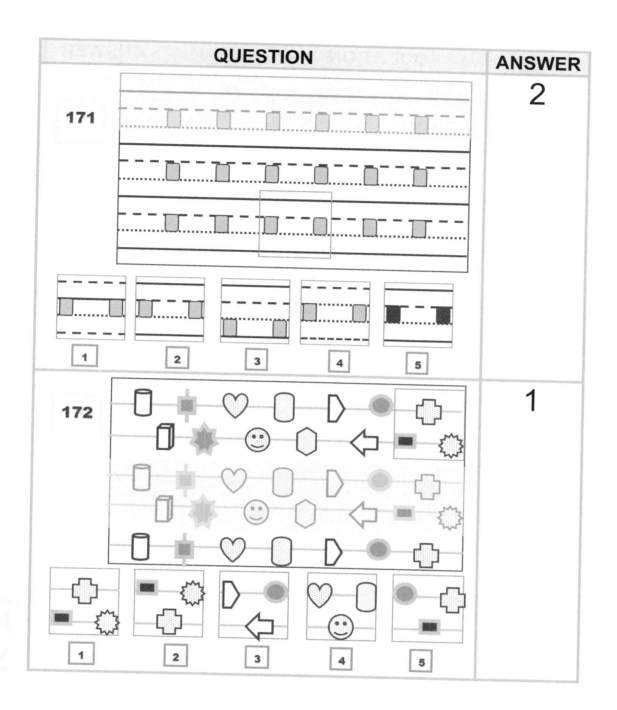

171 — Answer: **2**

172 — Answer: **1**

QUESTION	ANSWER

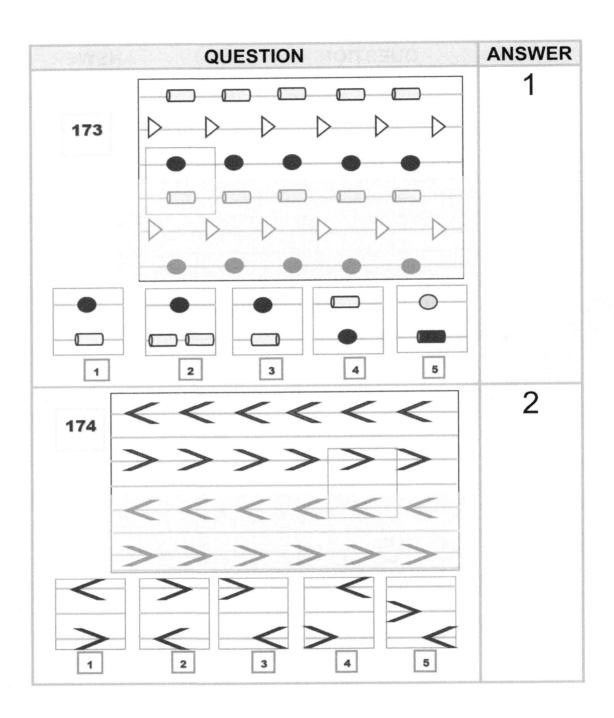

173

174

ANSWER 173: **1**

ANSWER 174: **2**

QUESTION	ANSWER
175 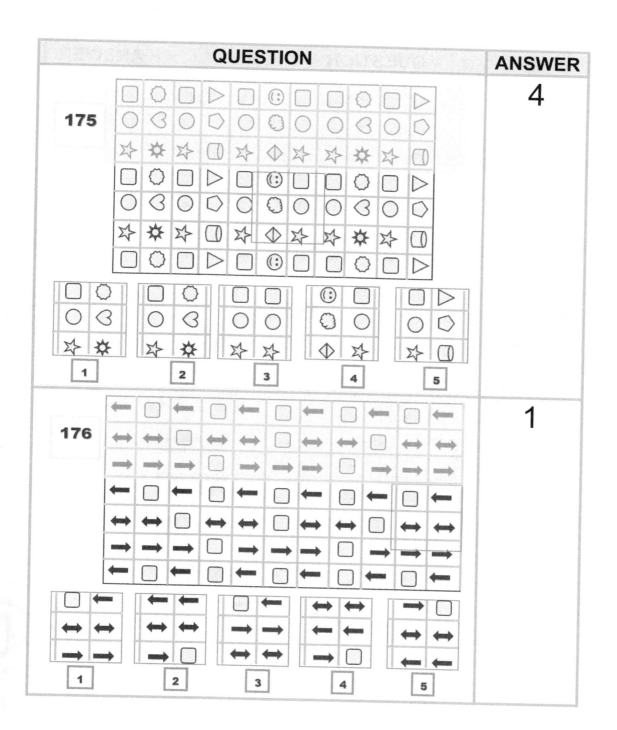	4
176	1

QUESTION	ANSWER

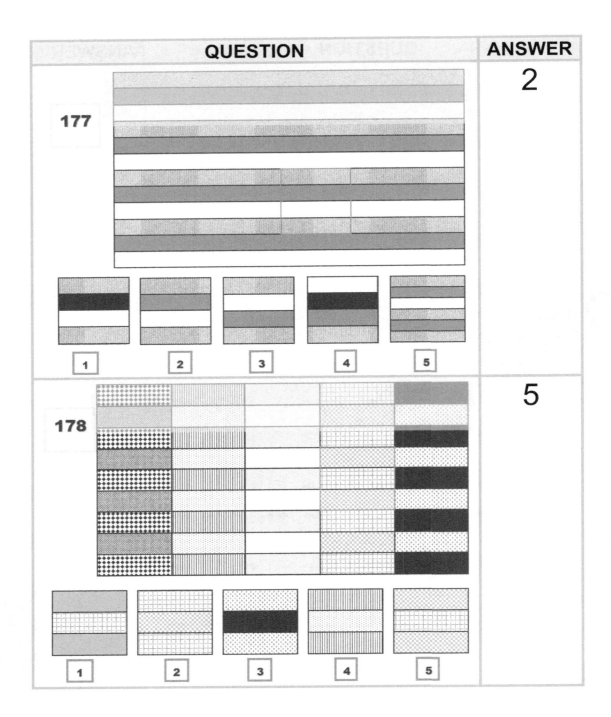

177 — Answer: 2

178 — Answer: 5

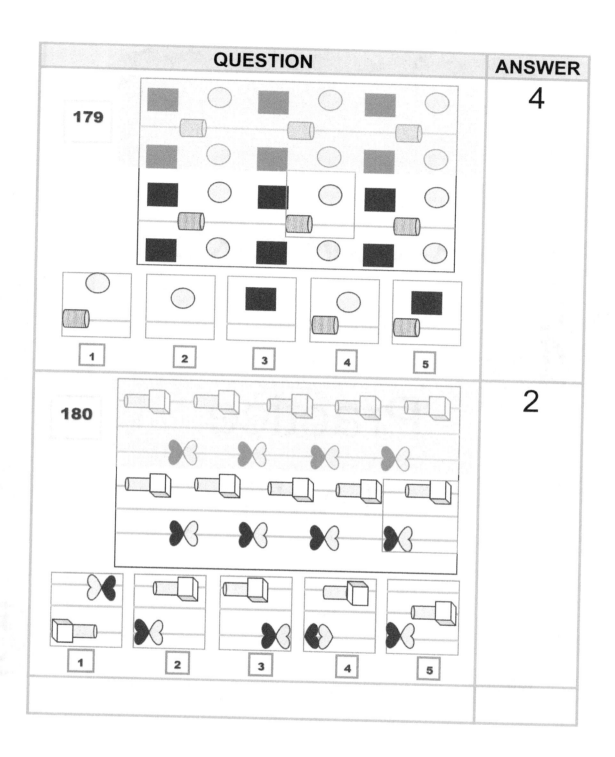

4

2

ANSWERS
to
Practice
Tests

PRACTICE TEST-1

QUESTION	ANSWER
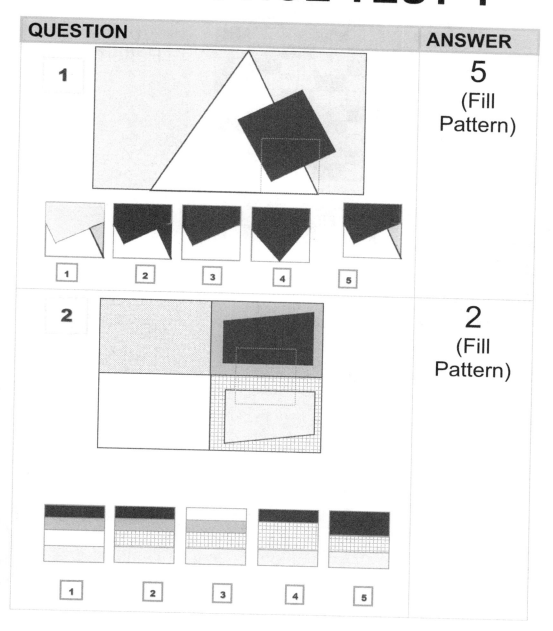	**5** (Fill Pattern)
	2 (Fill Pattern)

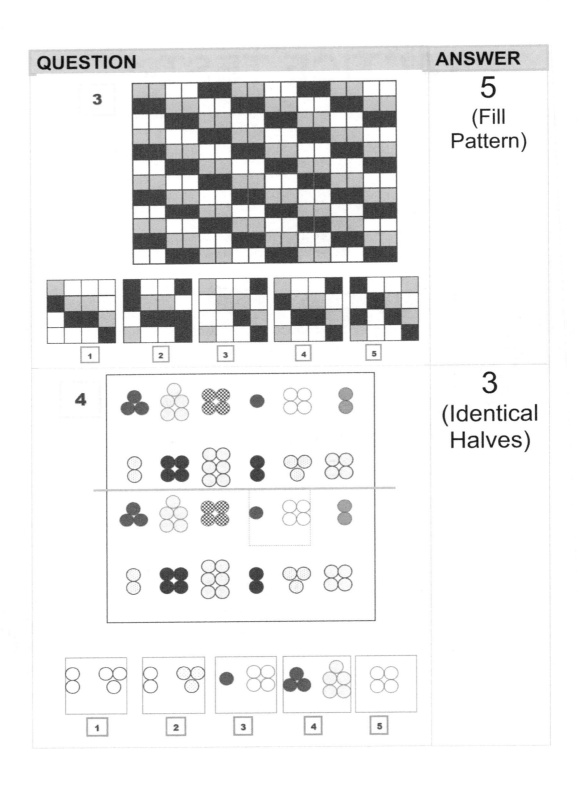

3

5
(Fill Pattern)

4

3
(Identical Halves)

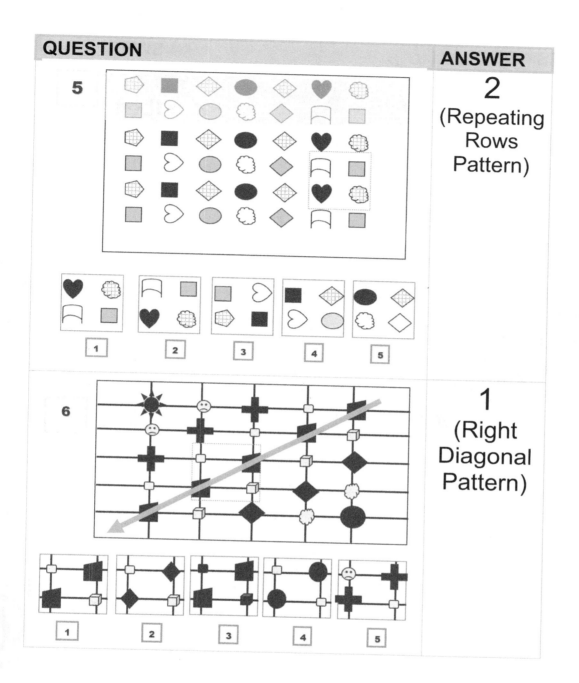

5 — **2** (Repeating Rows Pattern)

6 — **1** (Right Diagonal Pattern)

QUESTION	ANSWER
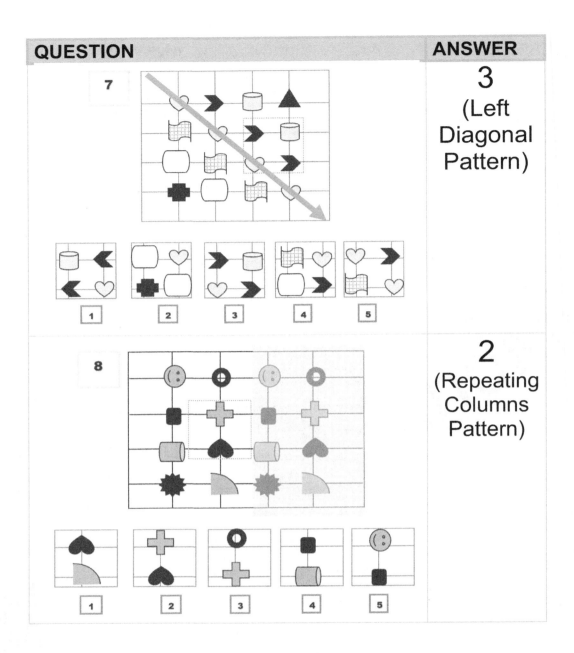	**3** (Left Diagonal Pattern) **2** (Repeating Columns Pattern)

QUESTION	ANSWER

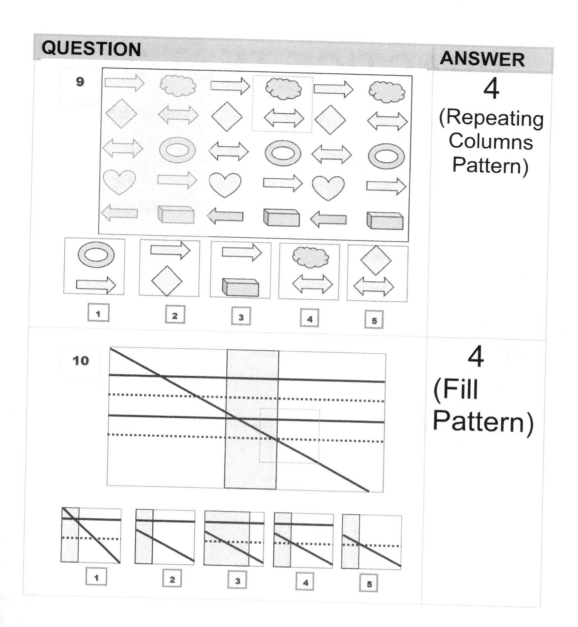

9

4
(Repeating Columns Pattern)

10

4
(Fill Pattern)

PRACTICE TEST-2

QUESTION	ANSWER
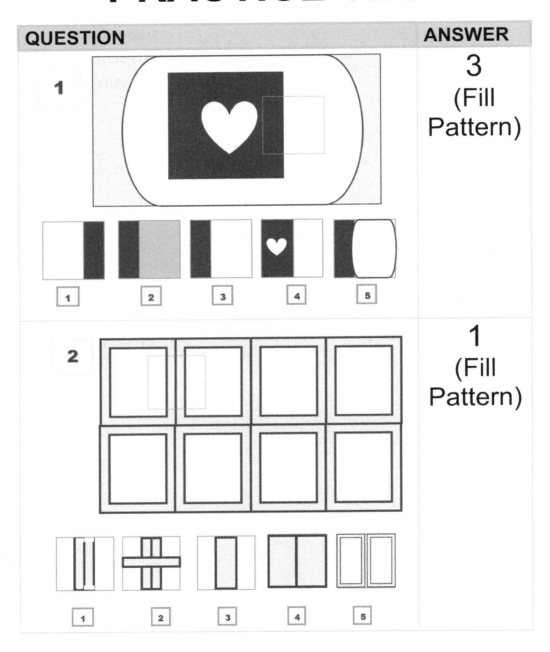	**3** (Fill Pattern) **1** (Fill Pattern)

QUESTION	ANSWER

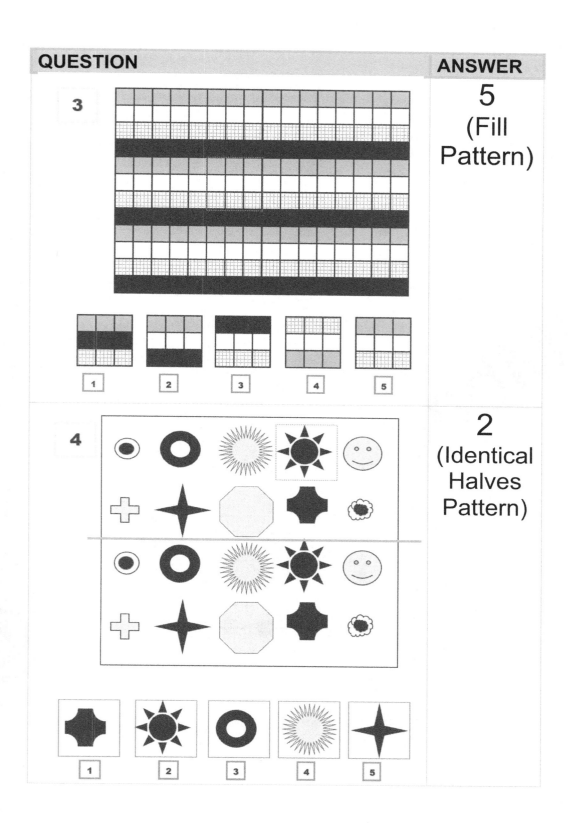

3

5
(Fill
Pattern)

4

2
(Identical
Halves
Pattern)

QUESTION	ANSWER

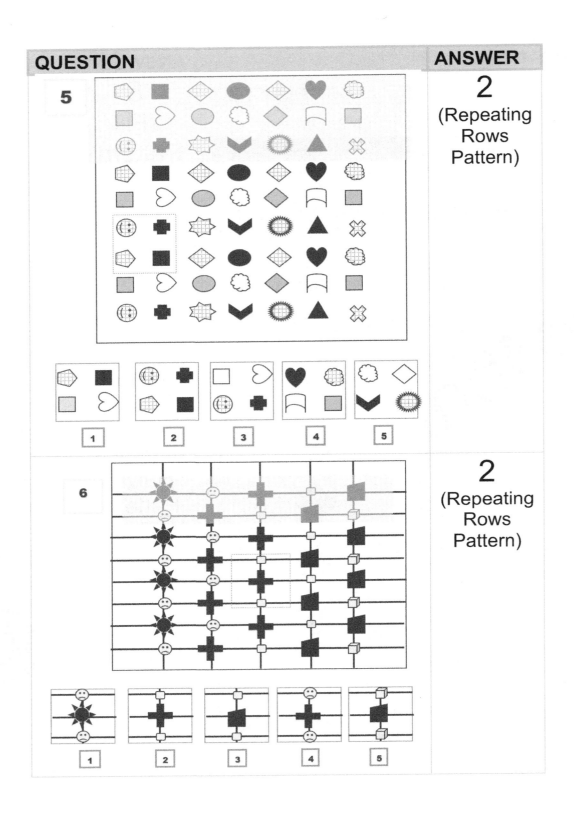

5

2
(Repeating Rows Pattern)

6

2
(Repeating Rows Pattern)

QUESTION	ANSWER
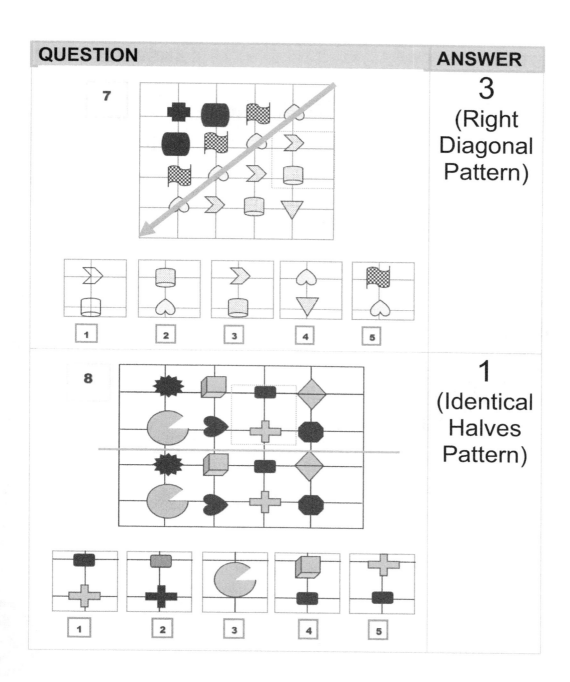	**3** (Right Diagonal Pattern)
	1 (Identical Halves Pattern)

QUESTION	ANSWER
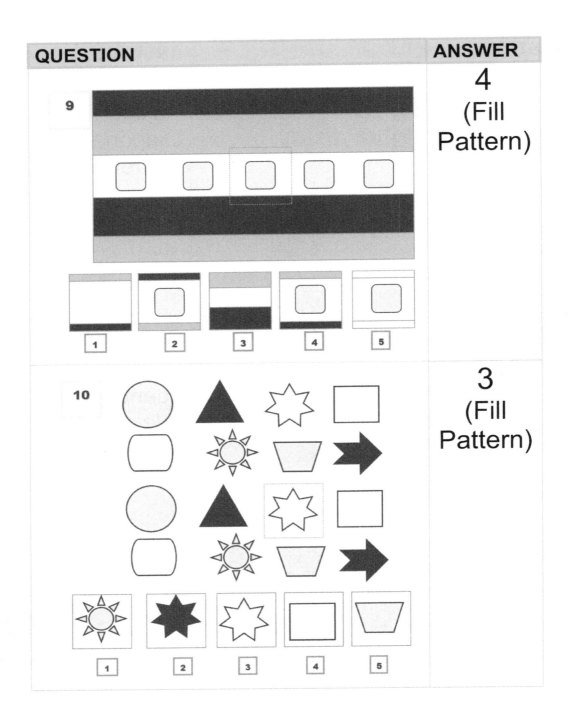	4 (Fill Pattern)
	3 (Fill Pattern)

Other ways to use this book

15 Mini Practice Tests

Questions are organized by each individual concept.
Picking 10-12 questions randomly and solving them out of
order serve as a mini practice test. **About 15 mini practice
tests** can be generated.

200+ Additional Questions

After solving each question, Write down the
answer in the box with **"?"**.

Now cover some other part of pattern with question
box. This will generate many additional questions.

Note: Additional questions Do Not have answer choices.

Question # 77

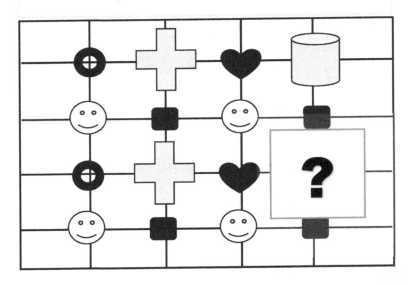

Generated from
Question # 77

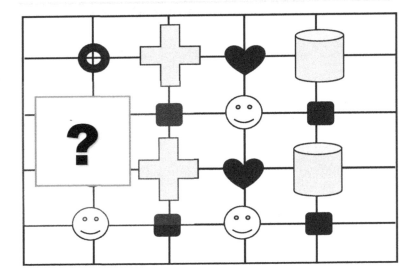

Question #14

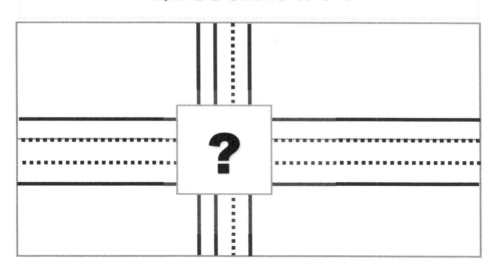

Generated from Question #14

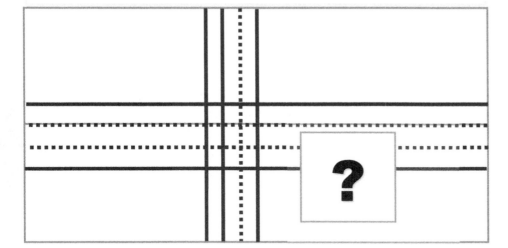

Additional Help

Have a question? You can reach author directly at
mindmineauthor@gmail.com

Made in the USA
Las Vegas, NV
28 October 2022